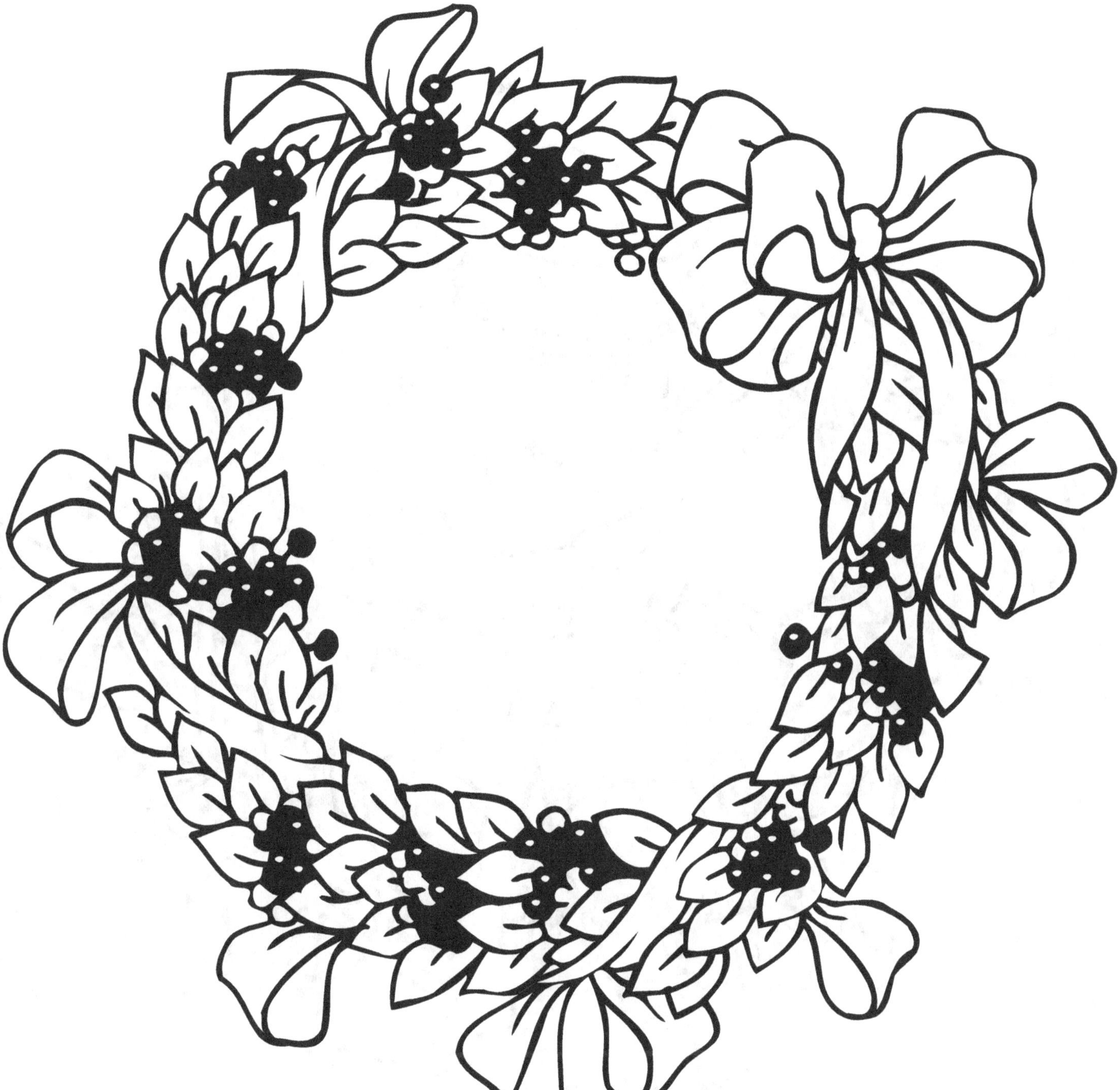

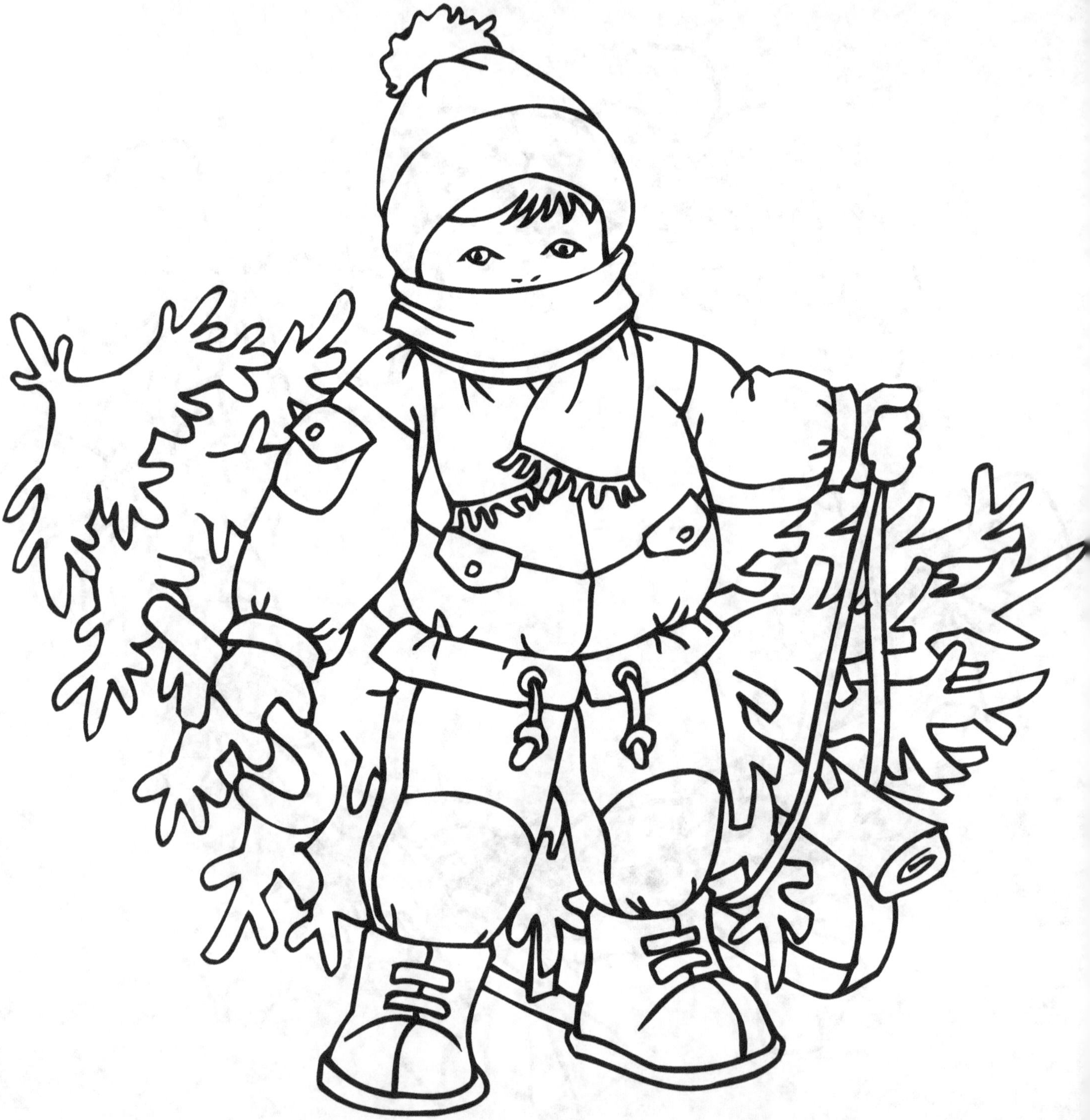

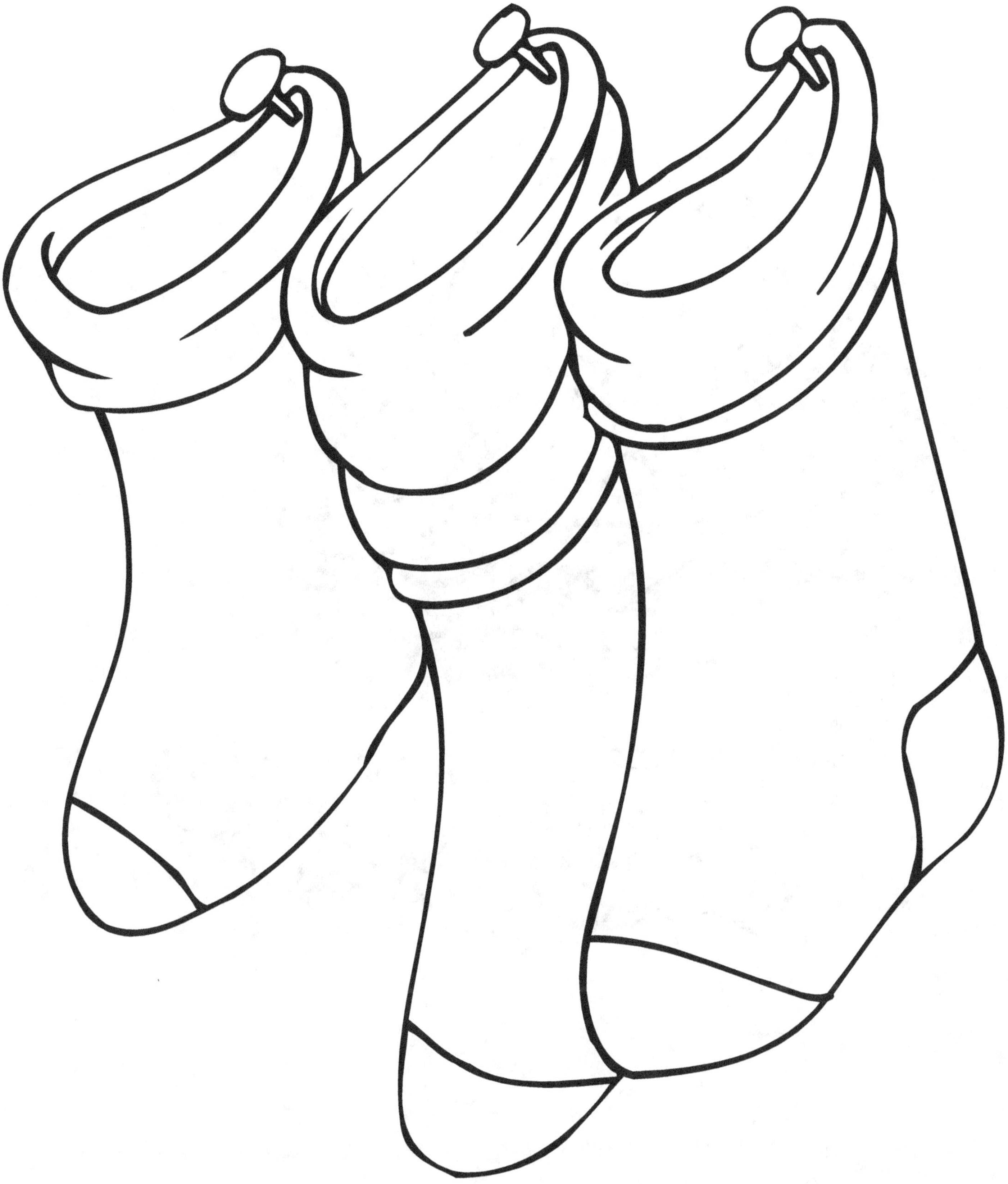

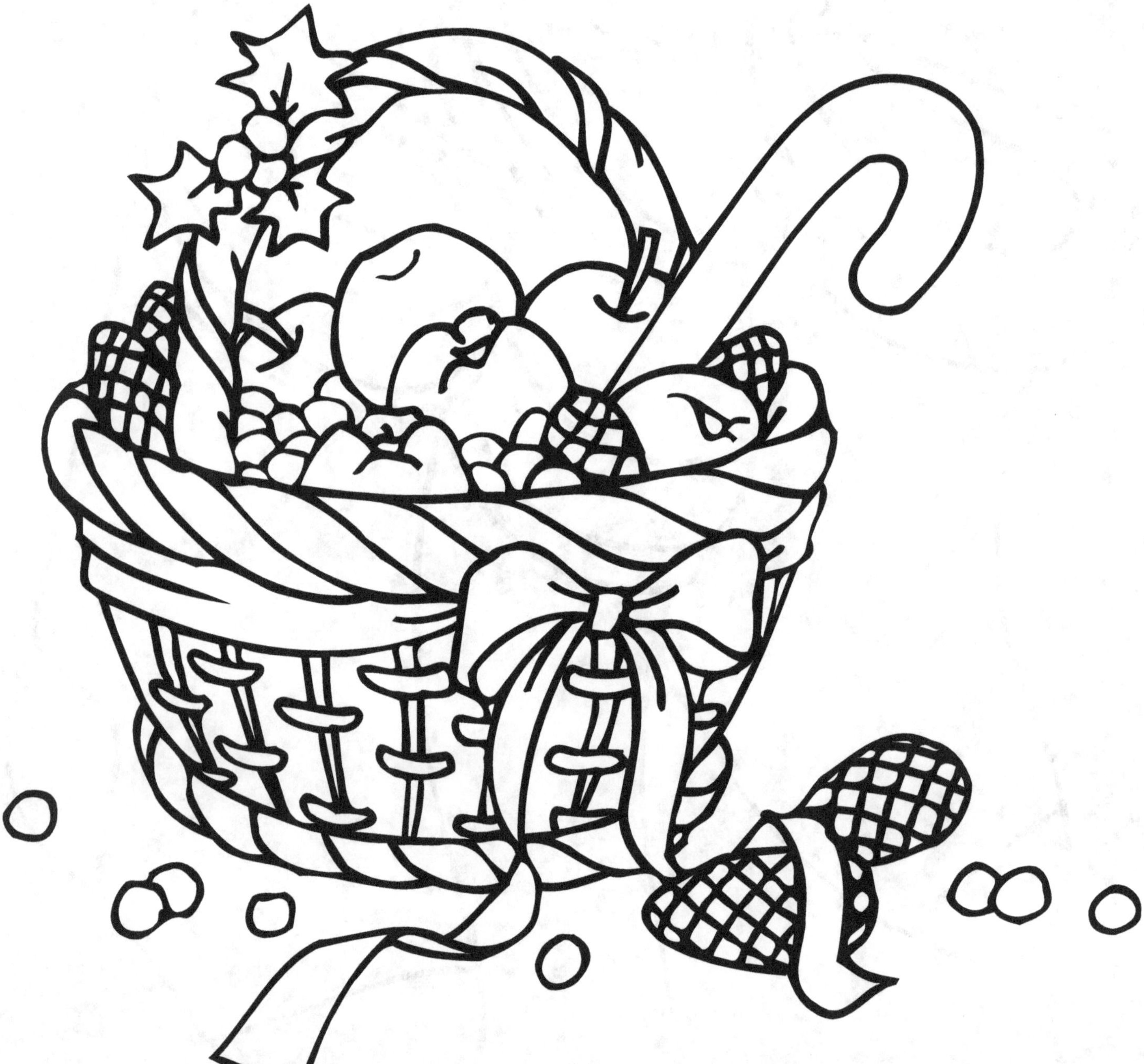

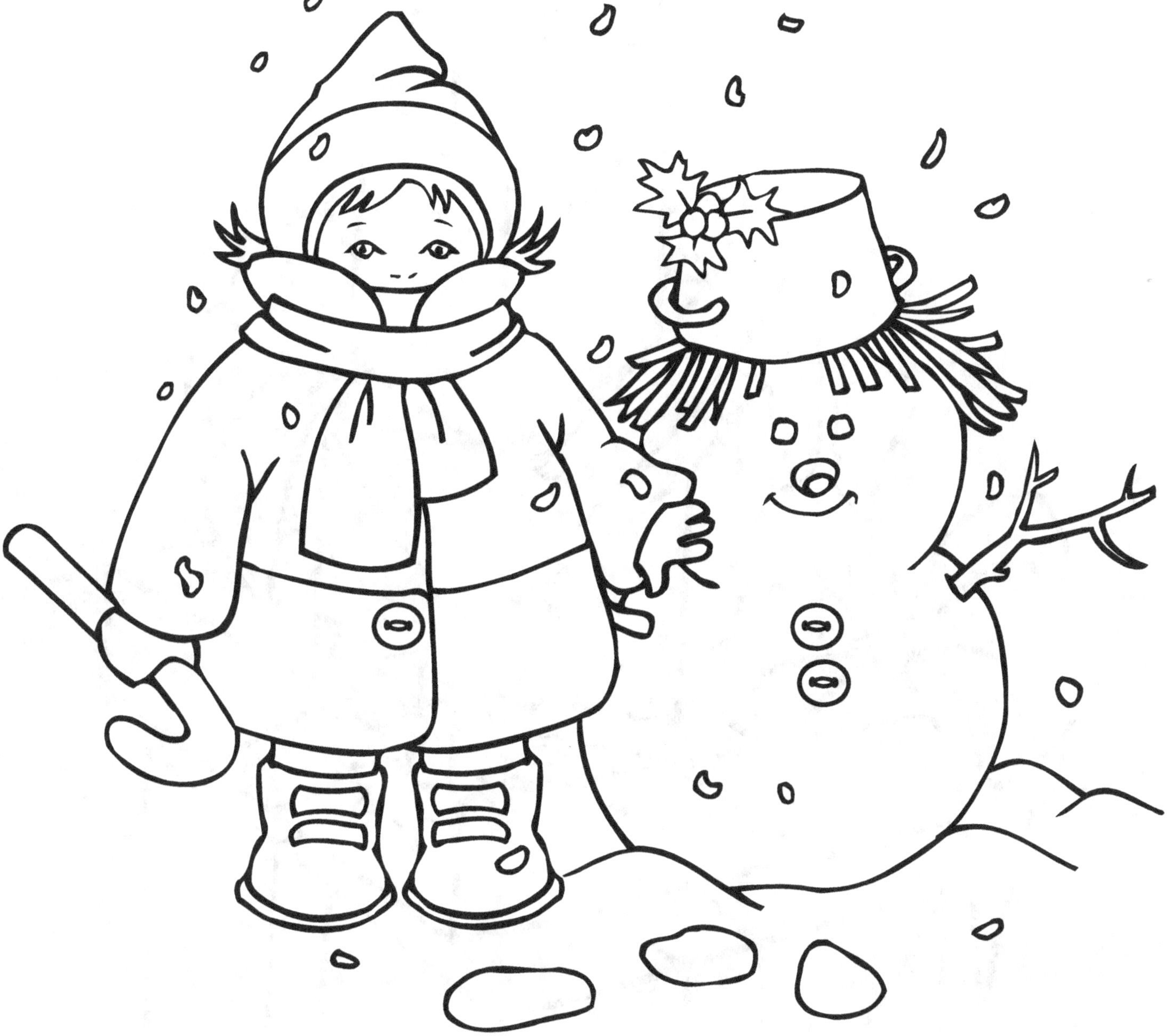

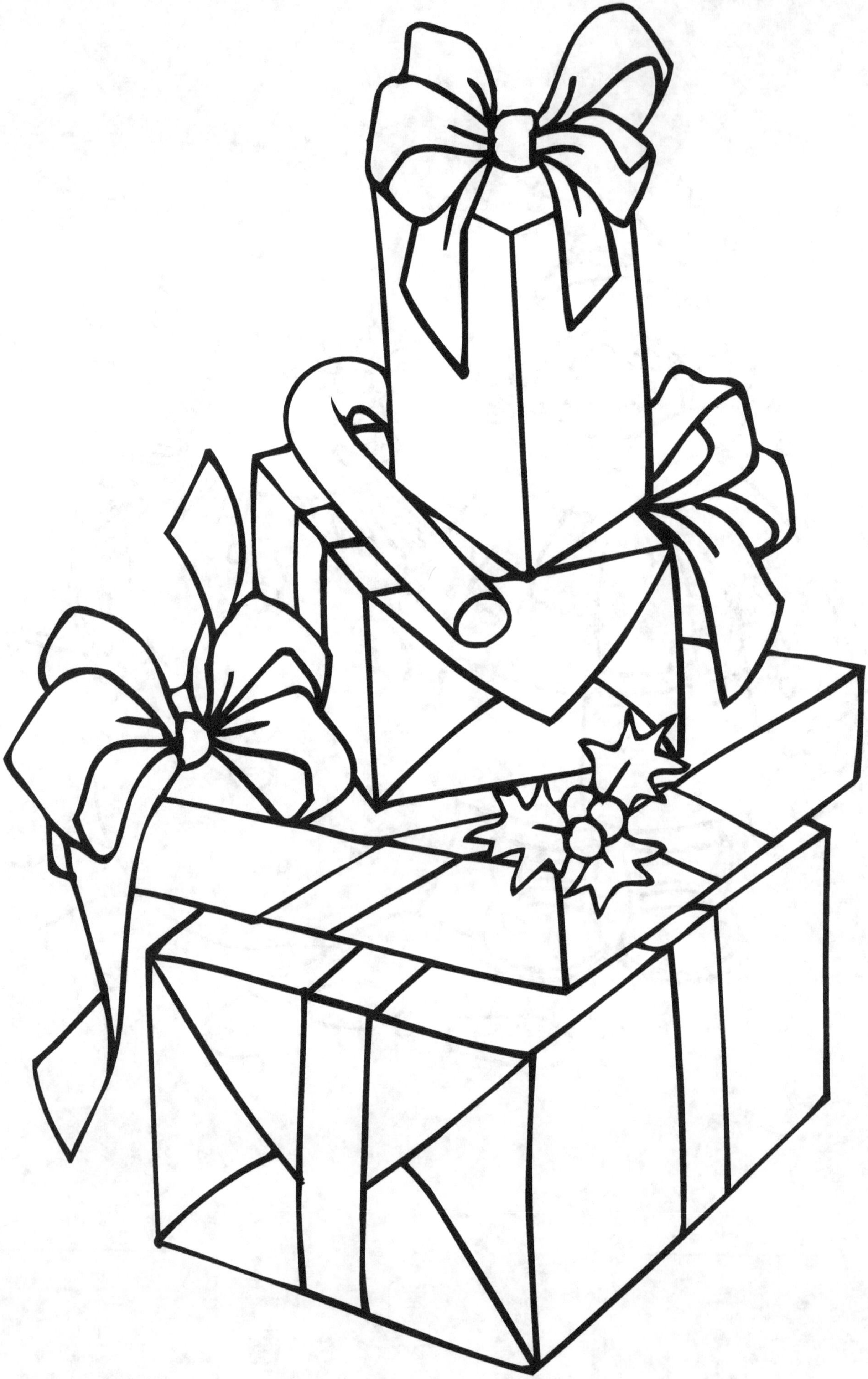

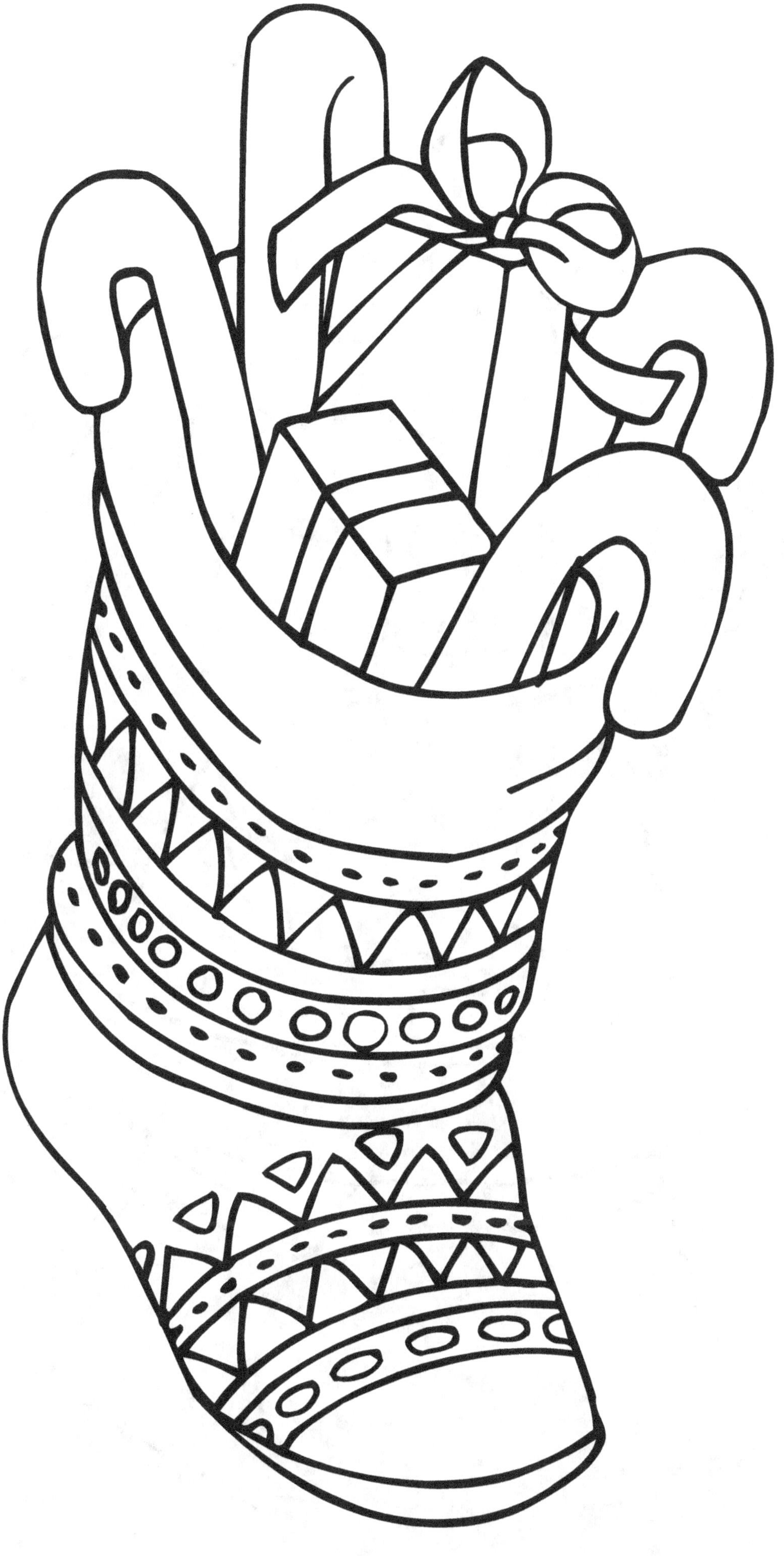

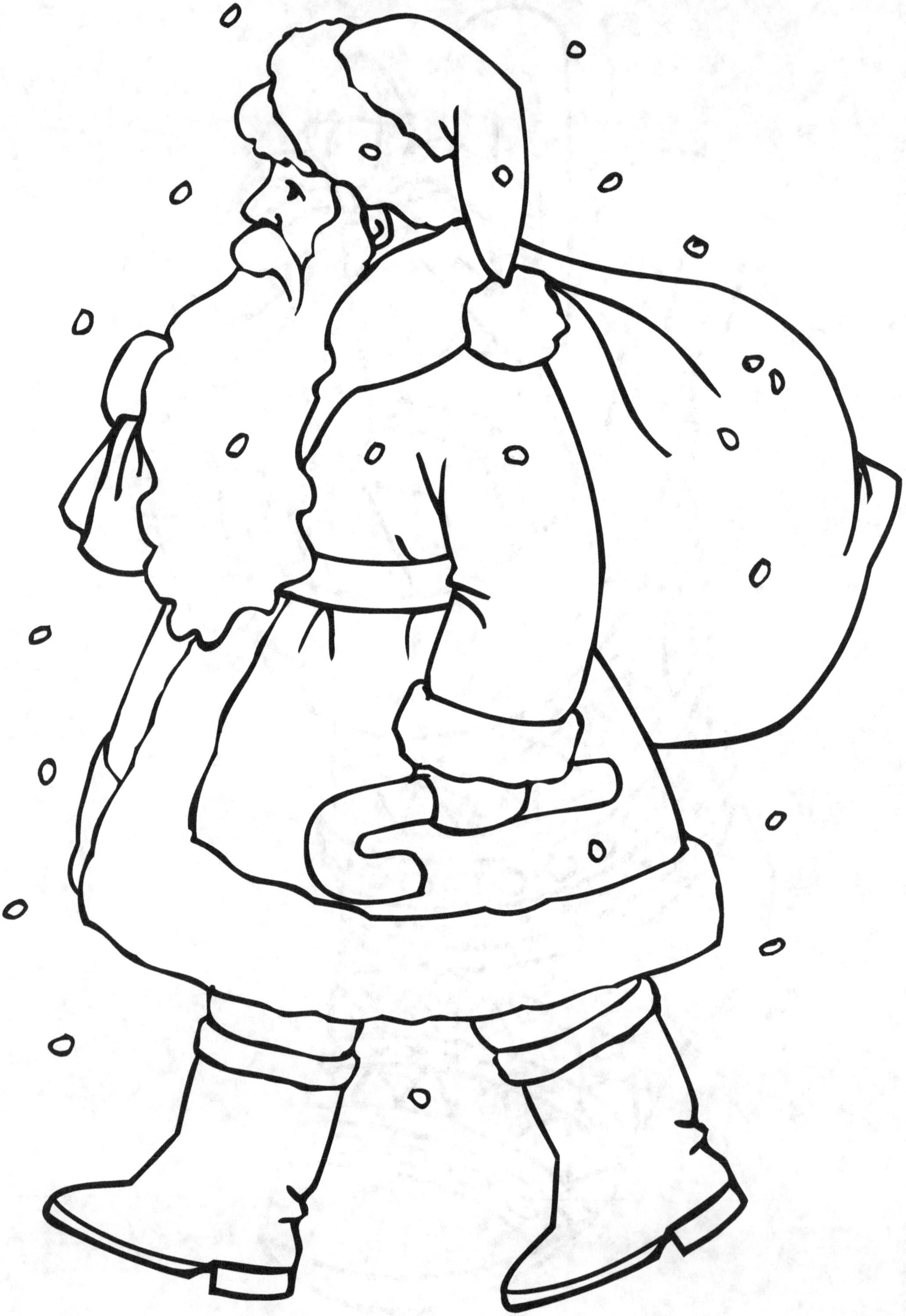

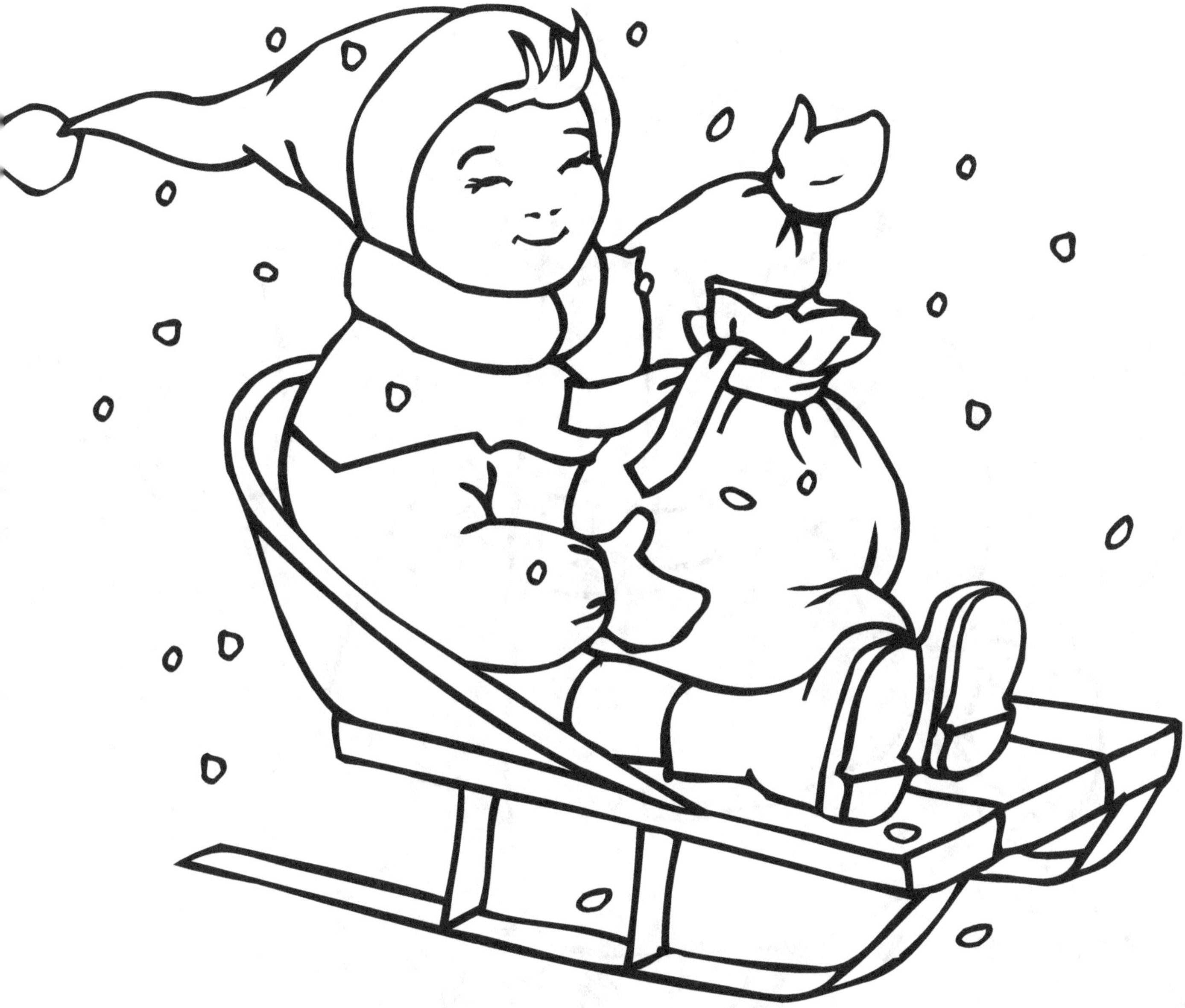

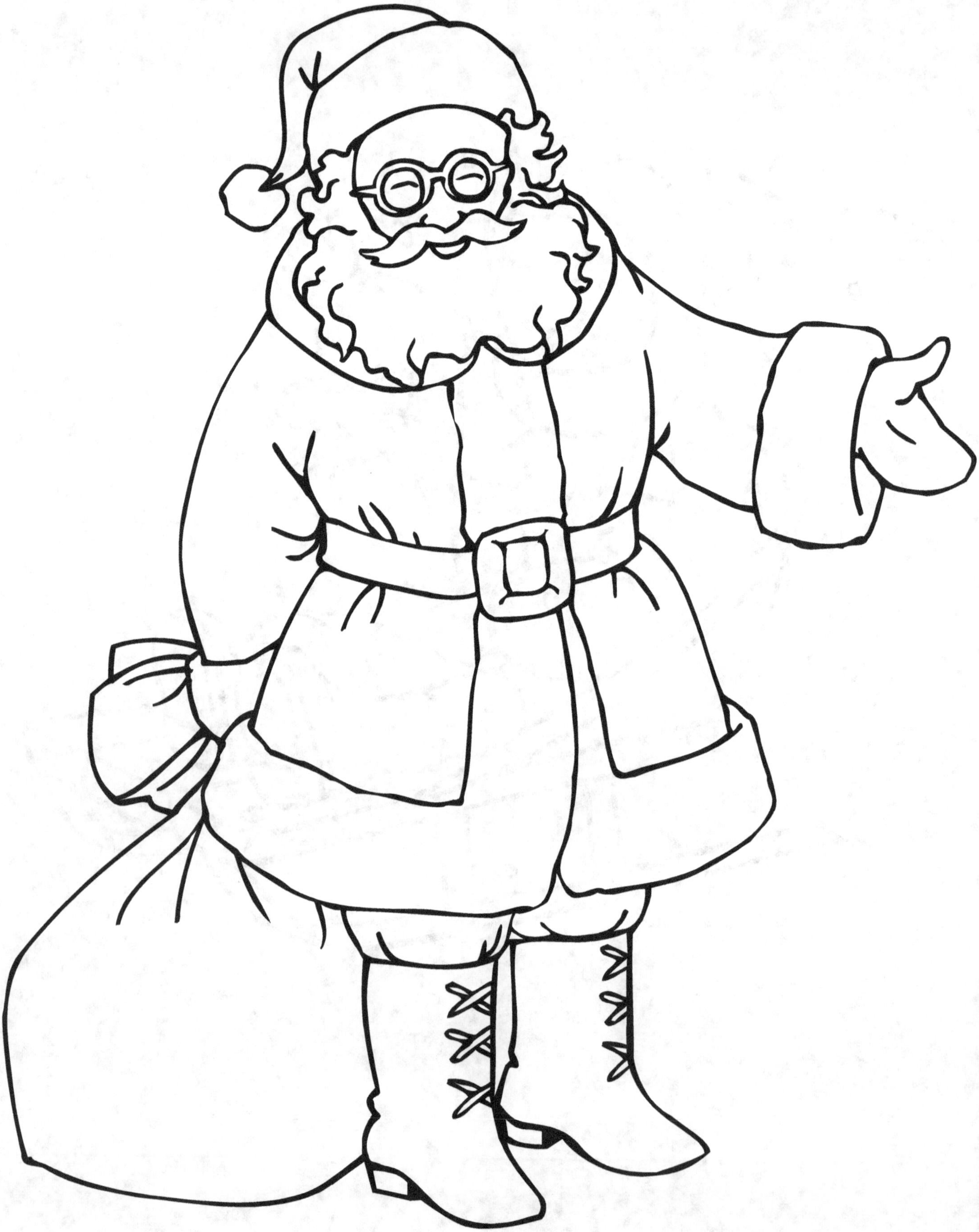

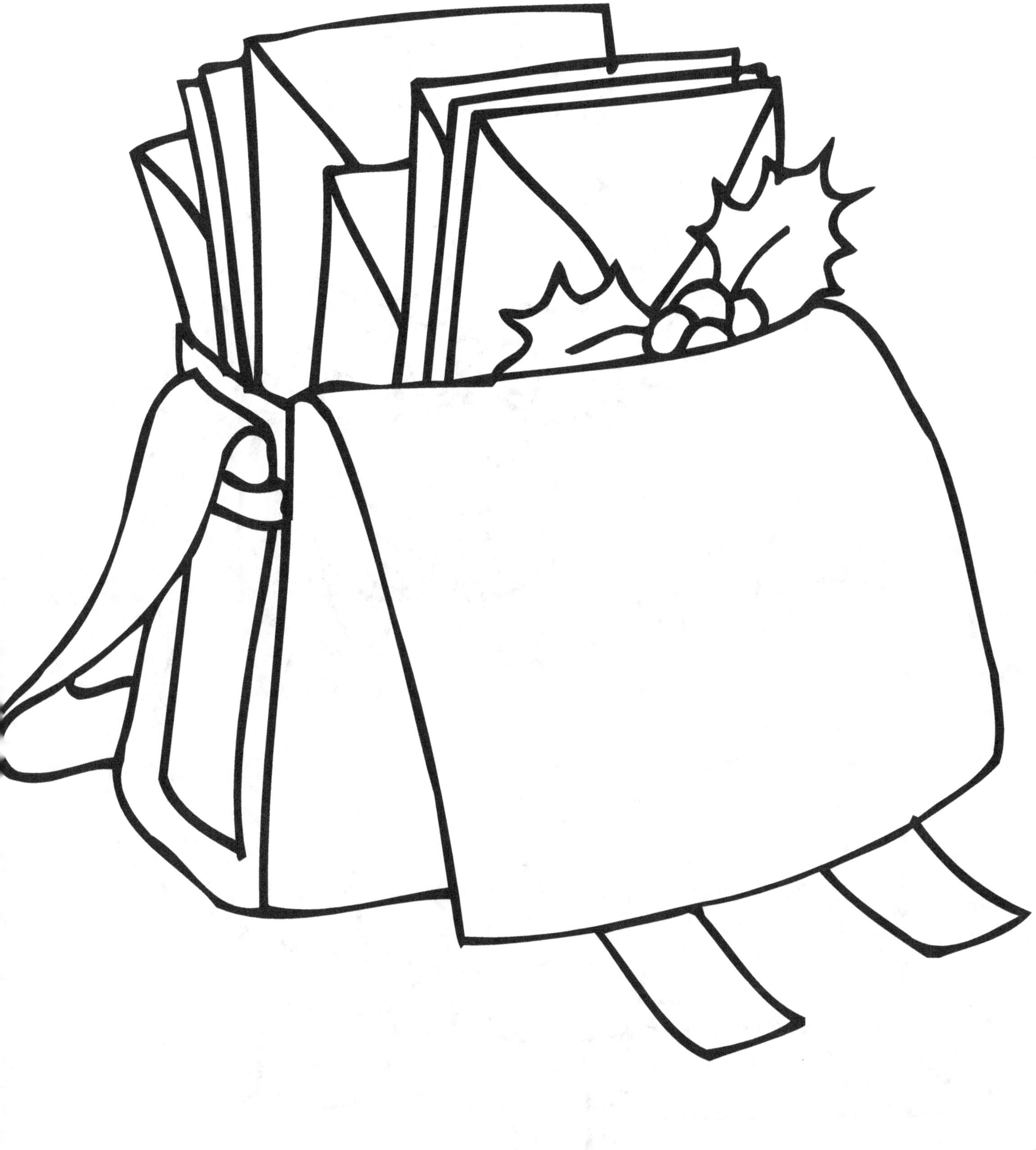

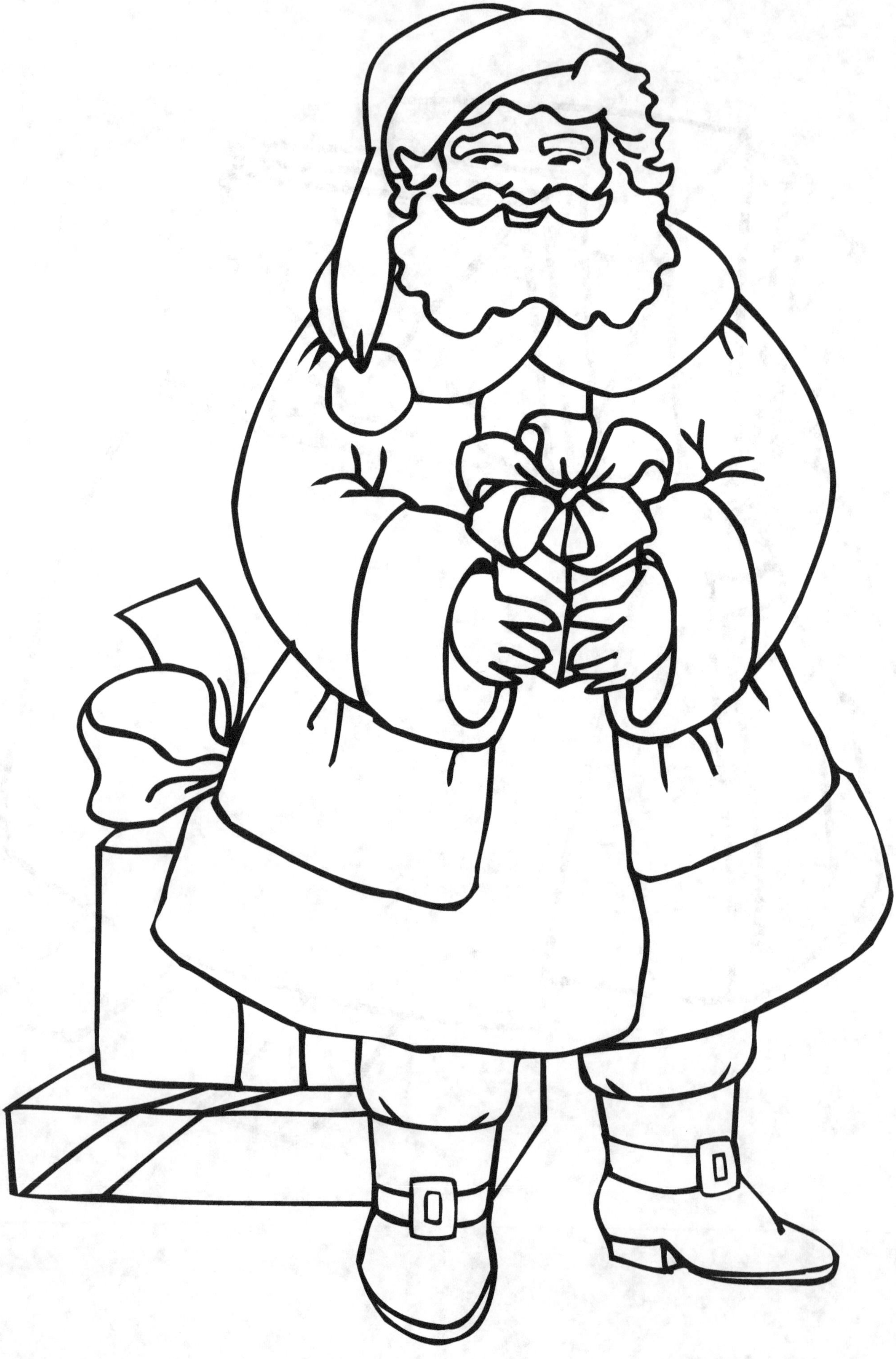

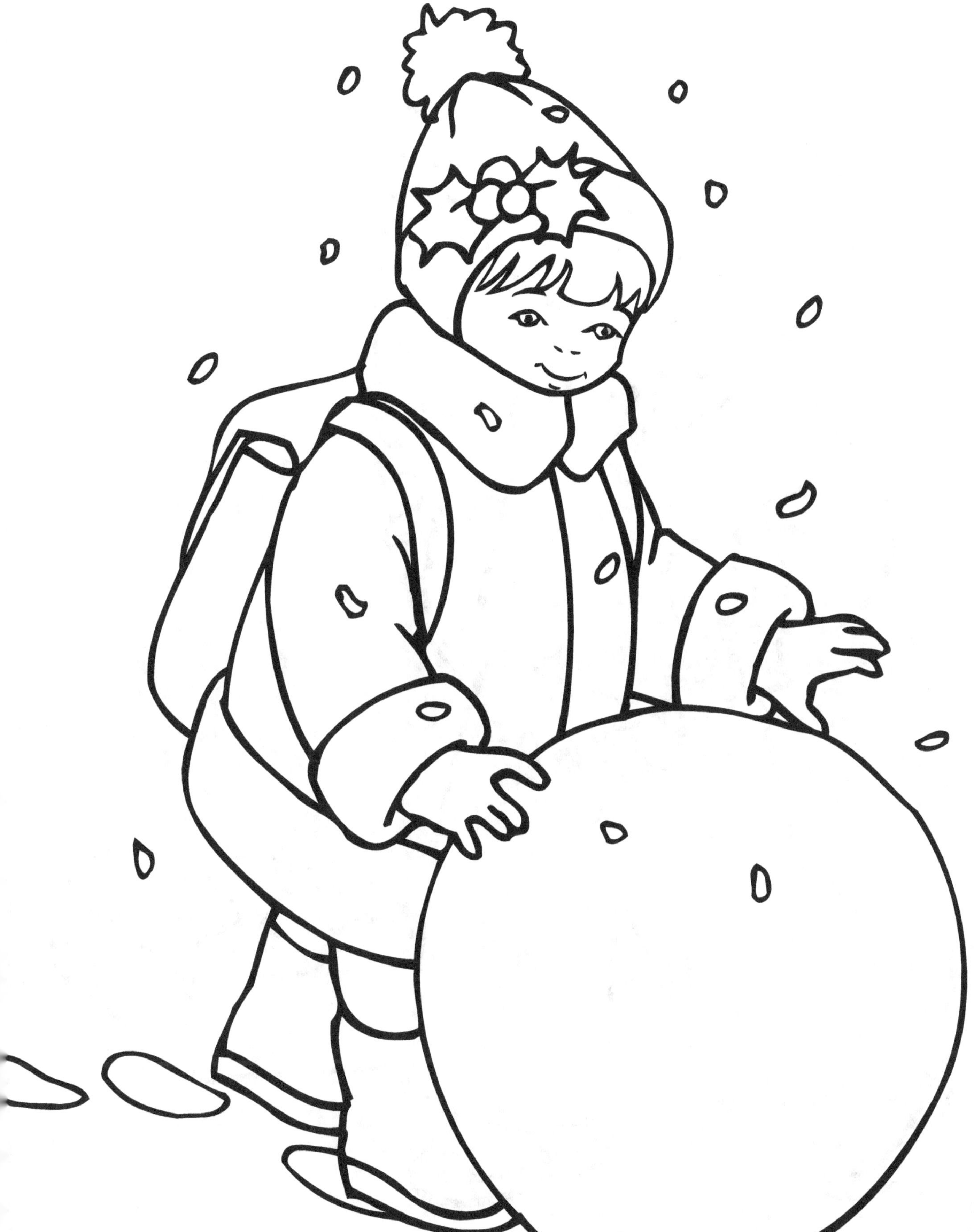

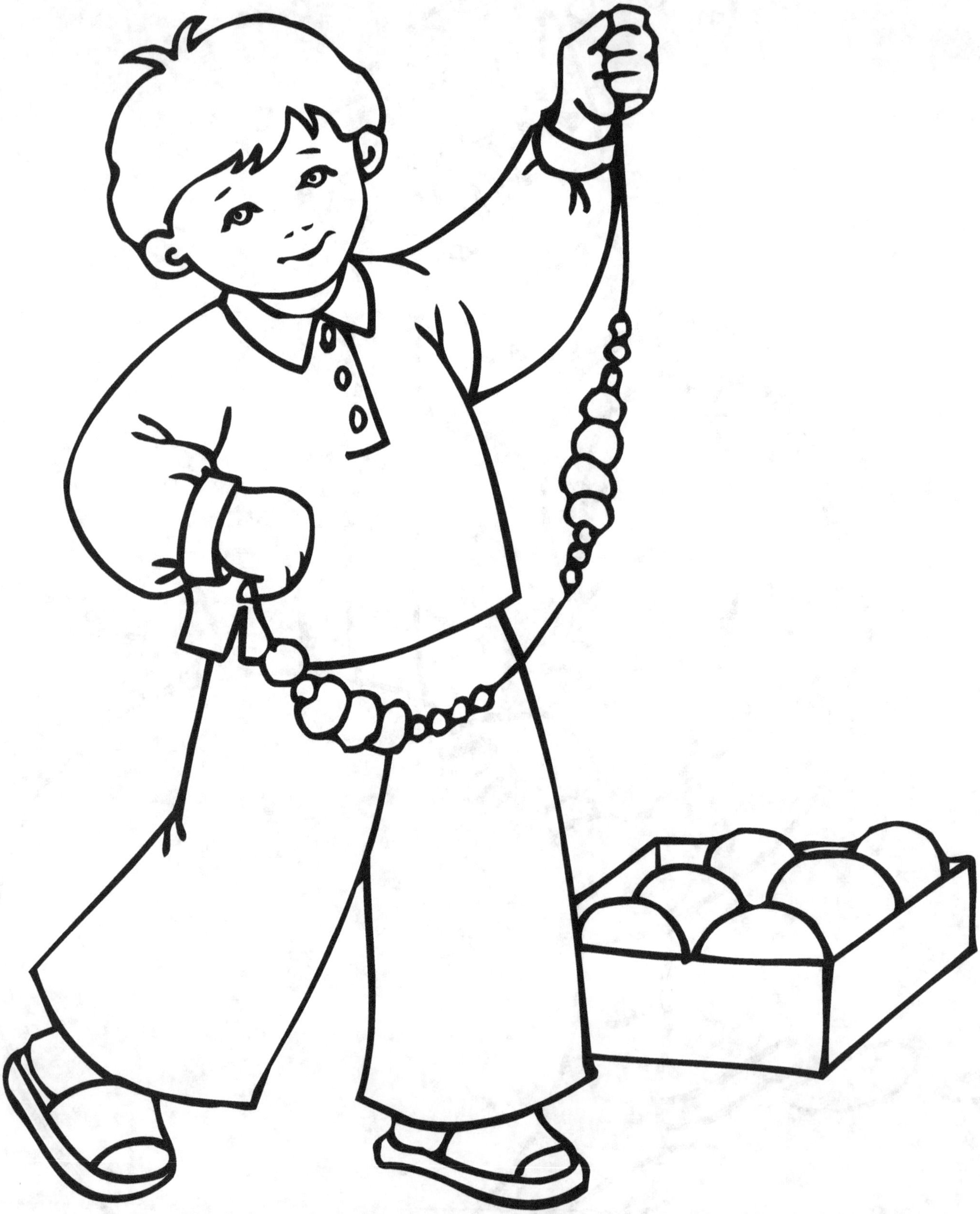

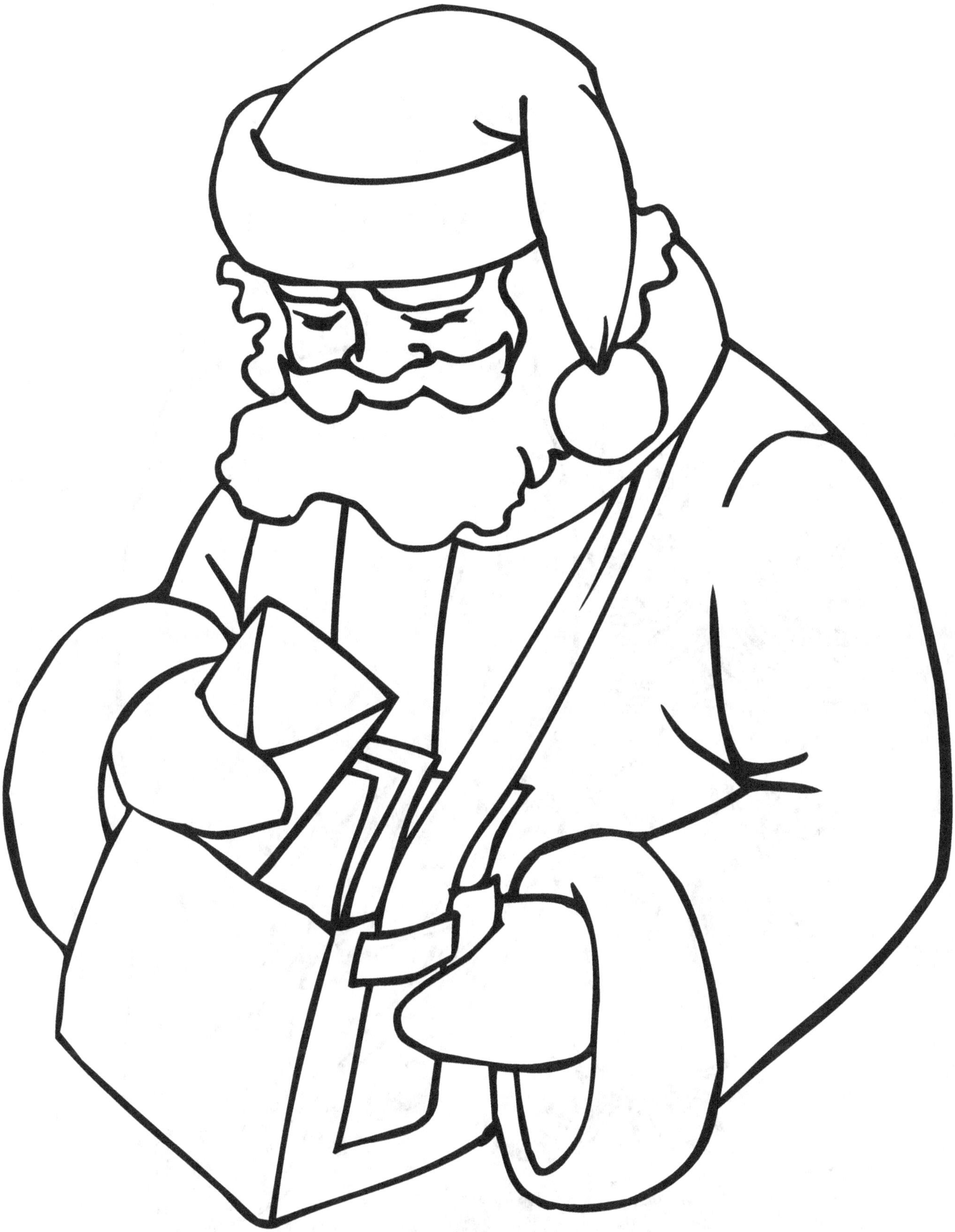

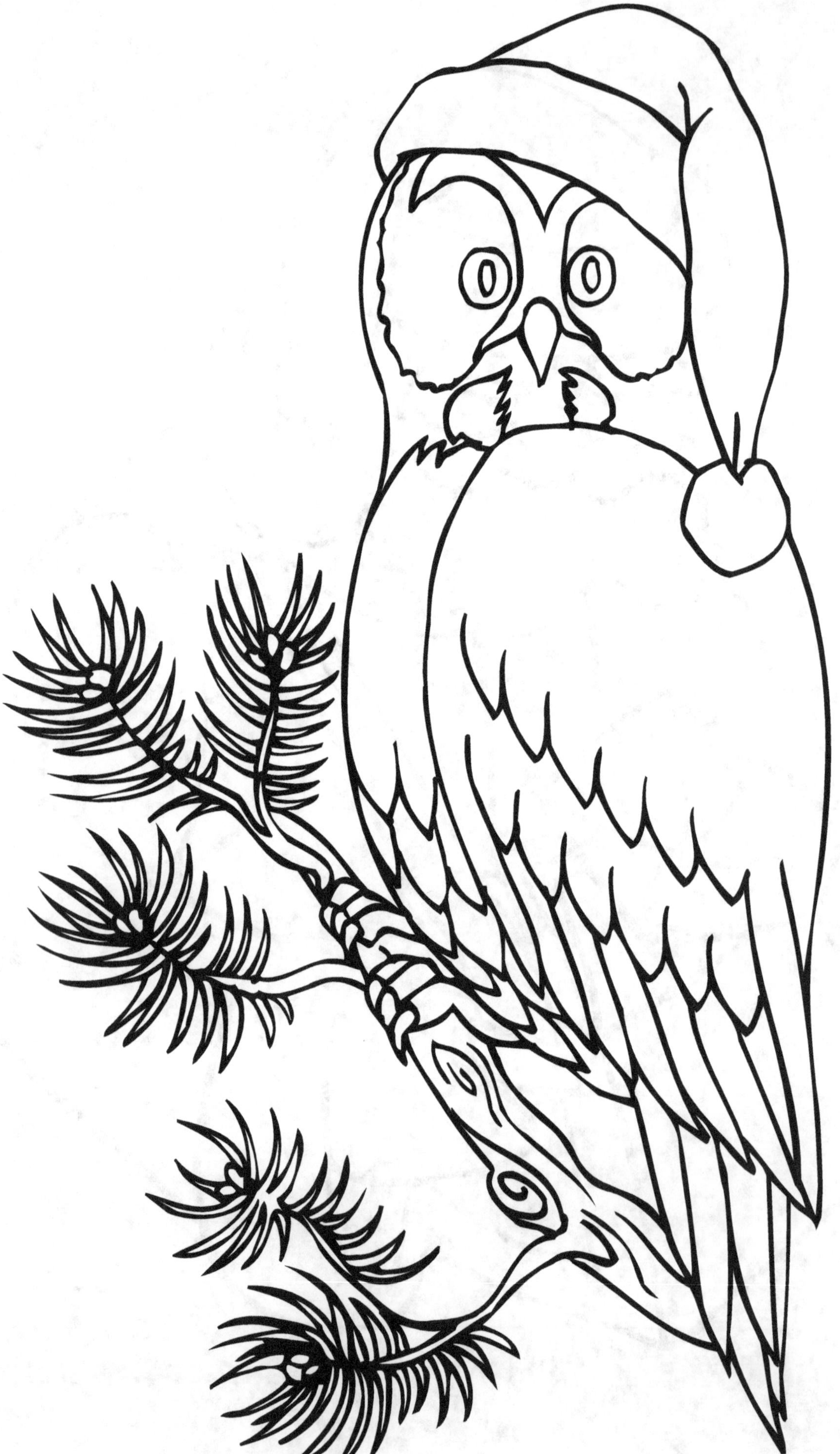

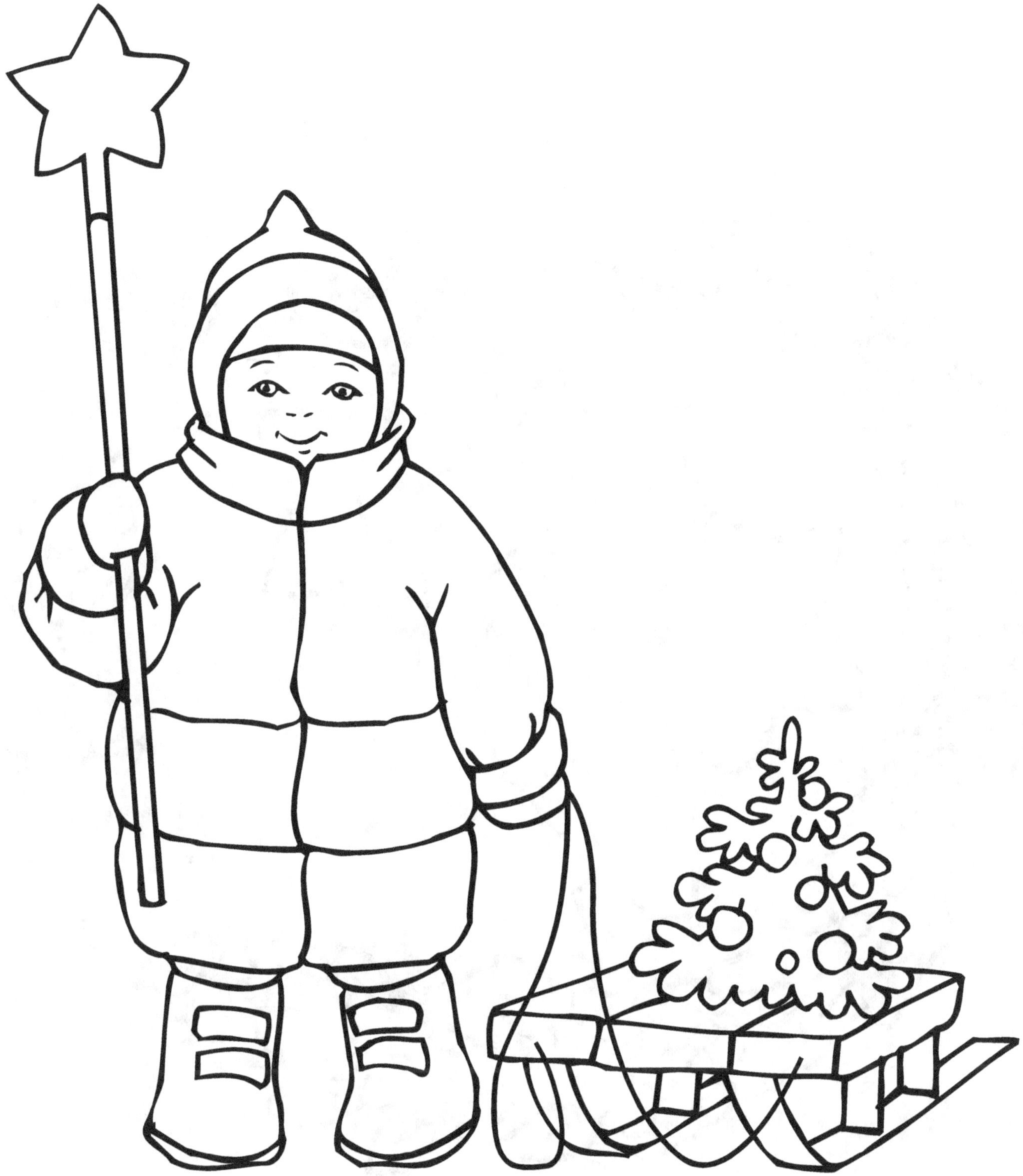

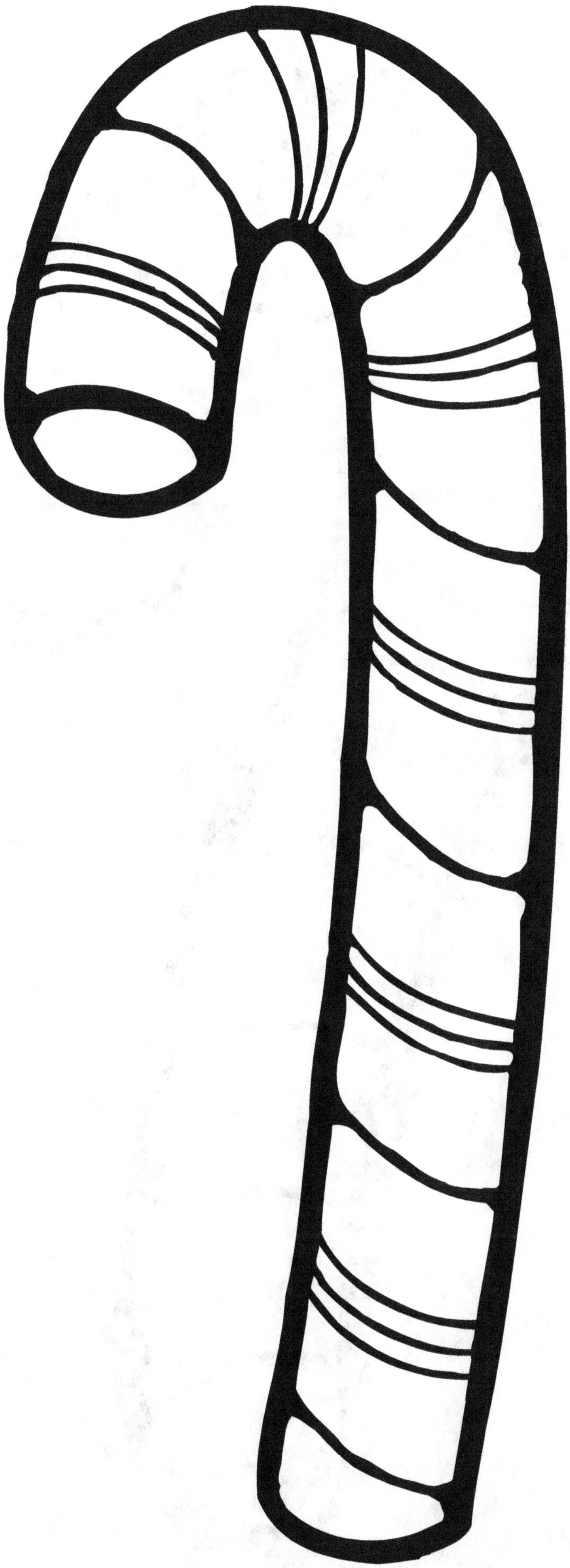

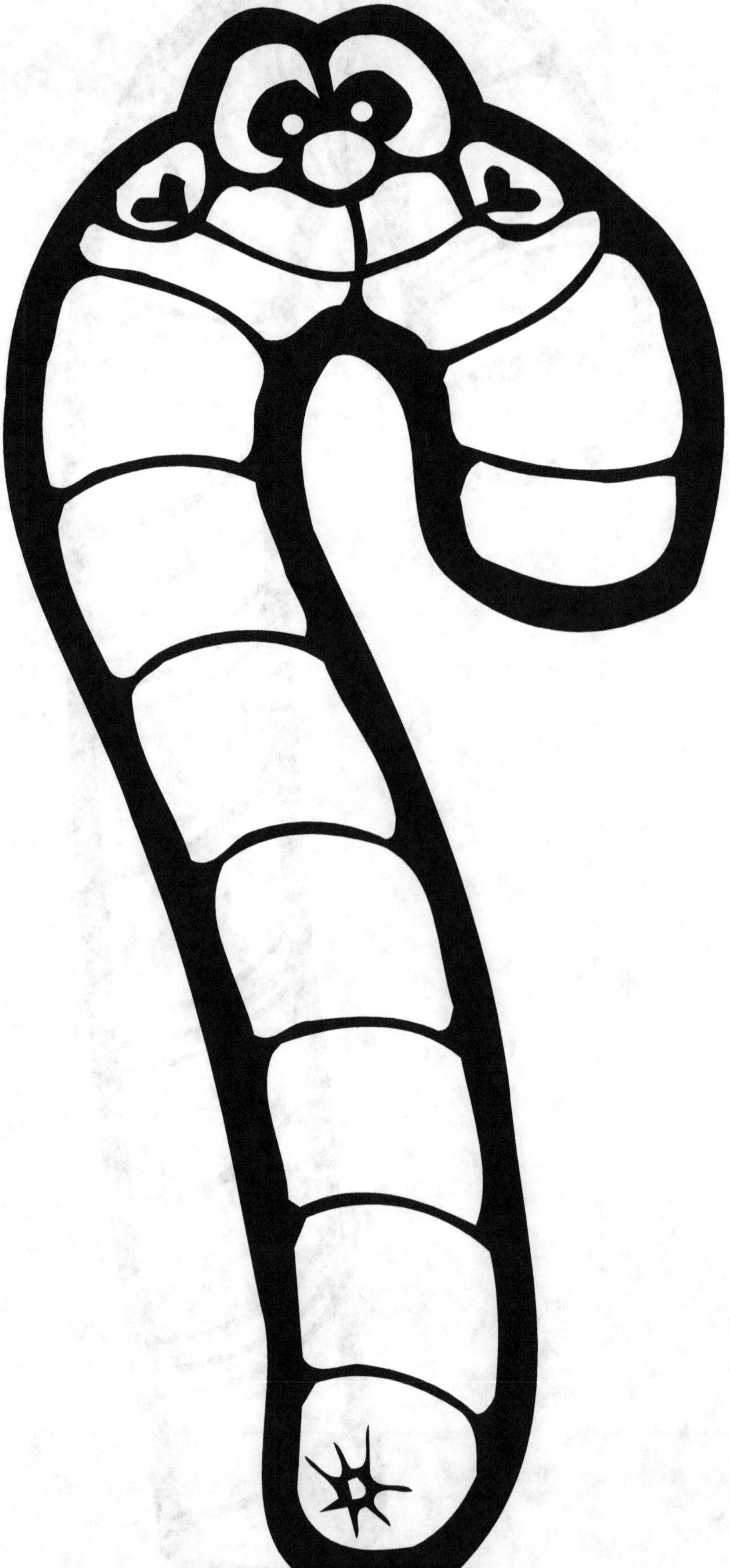

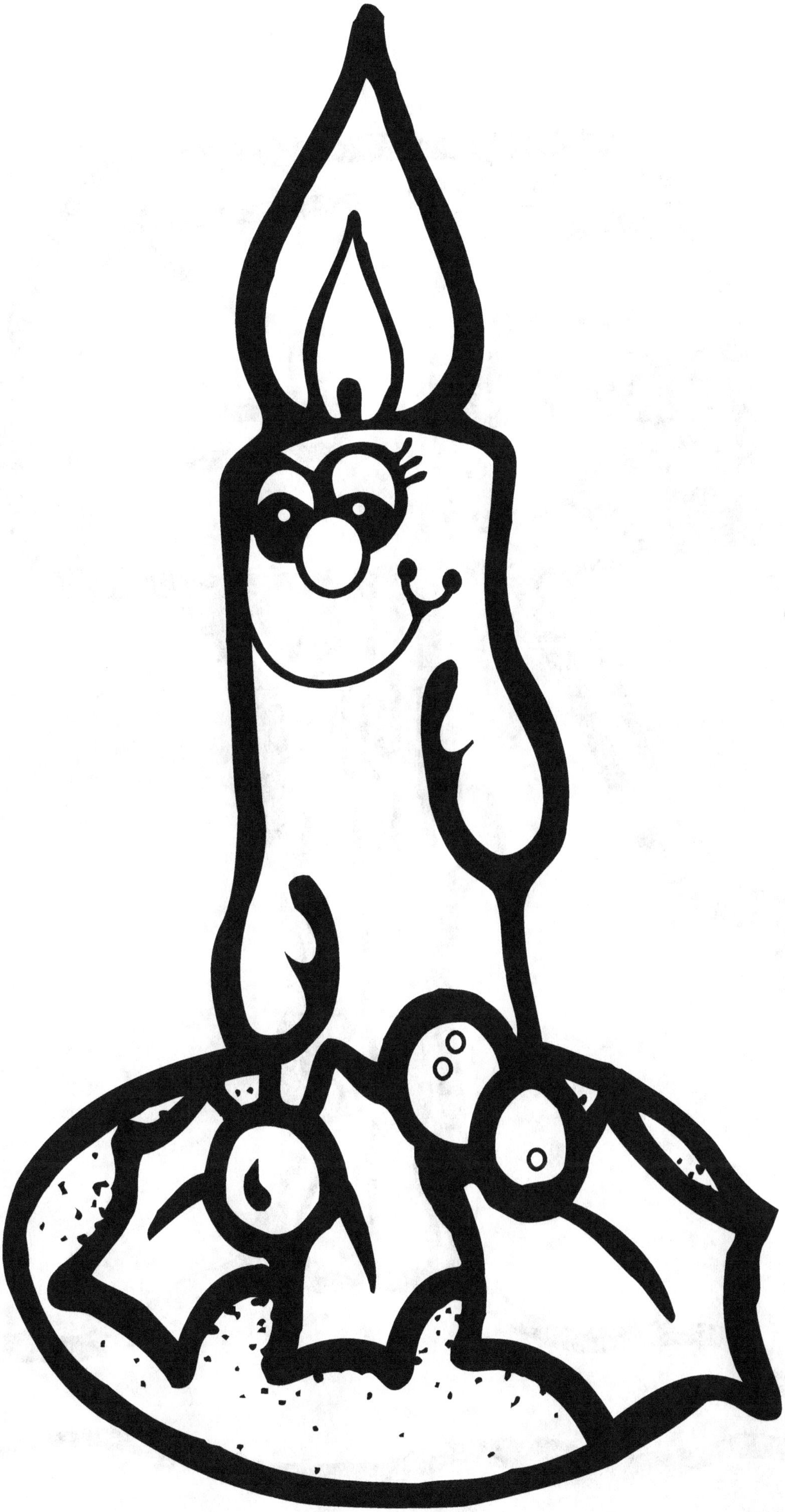

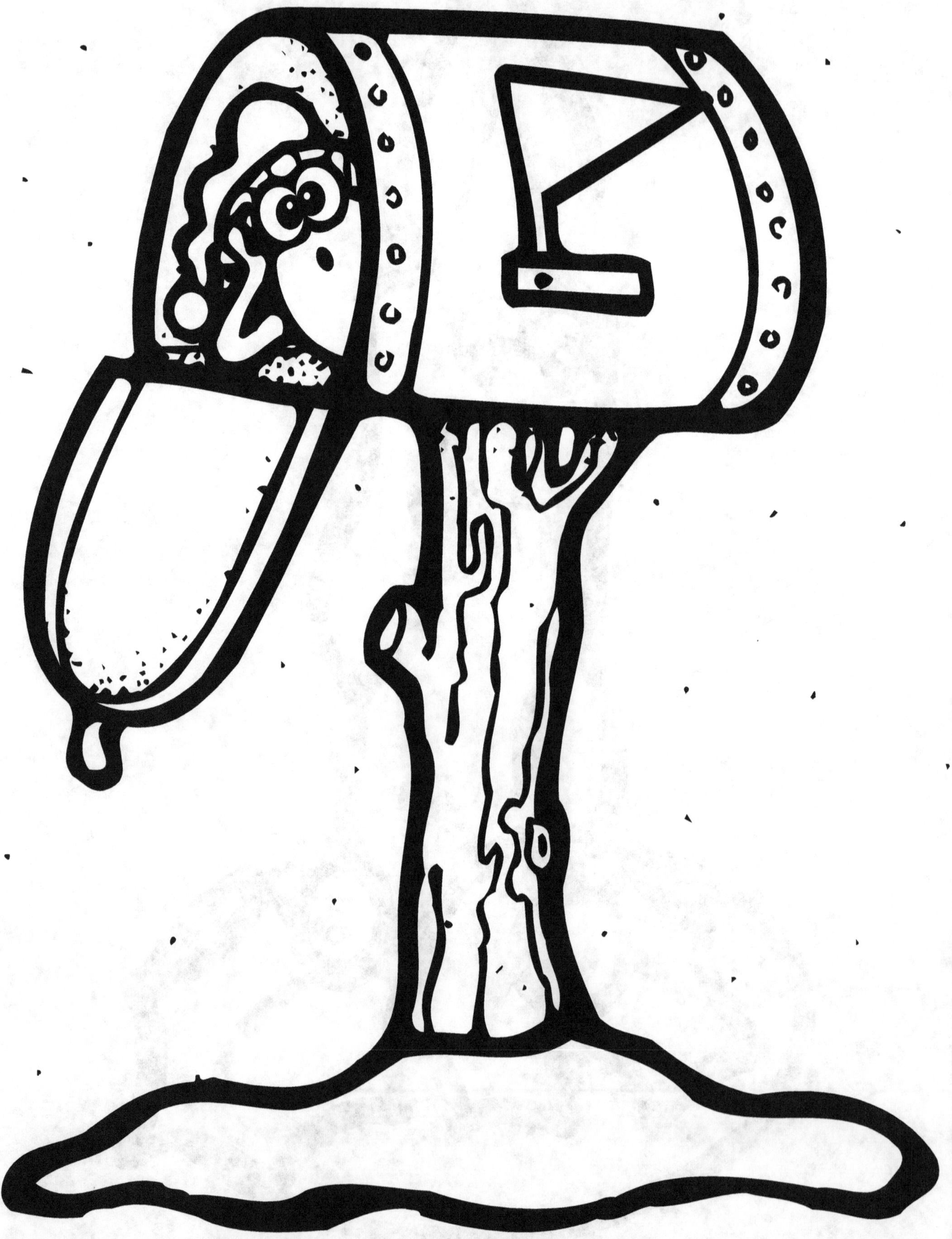

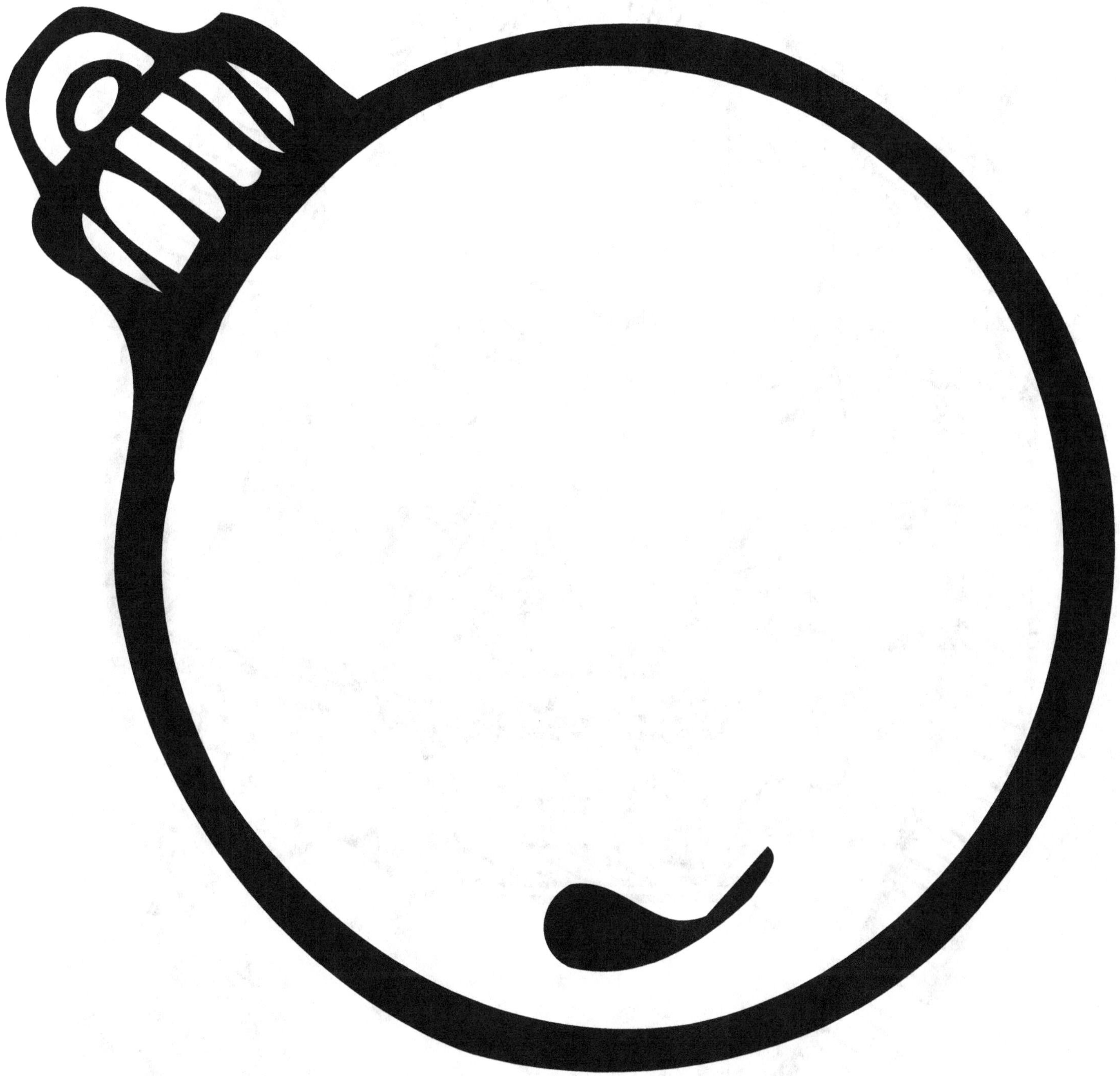

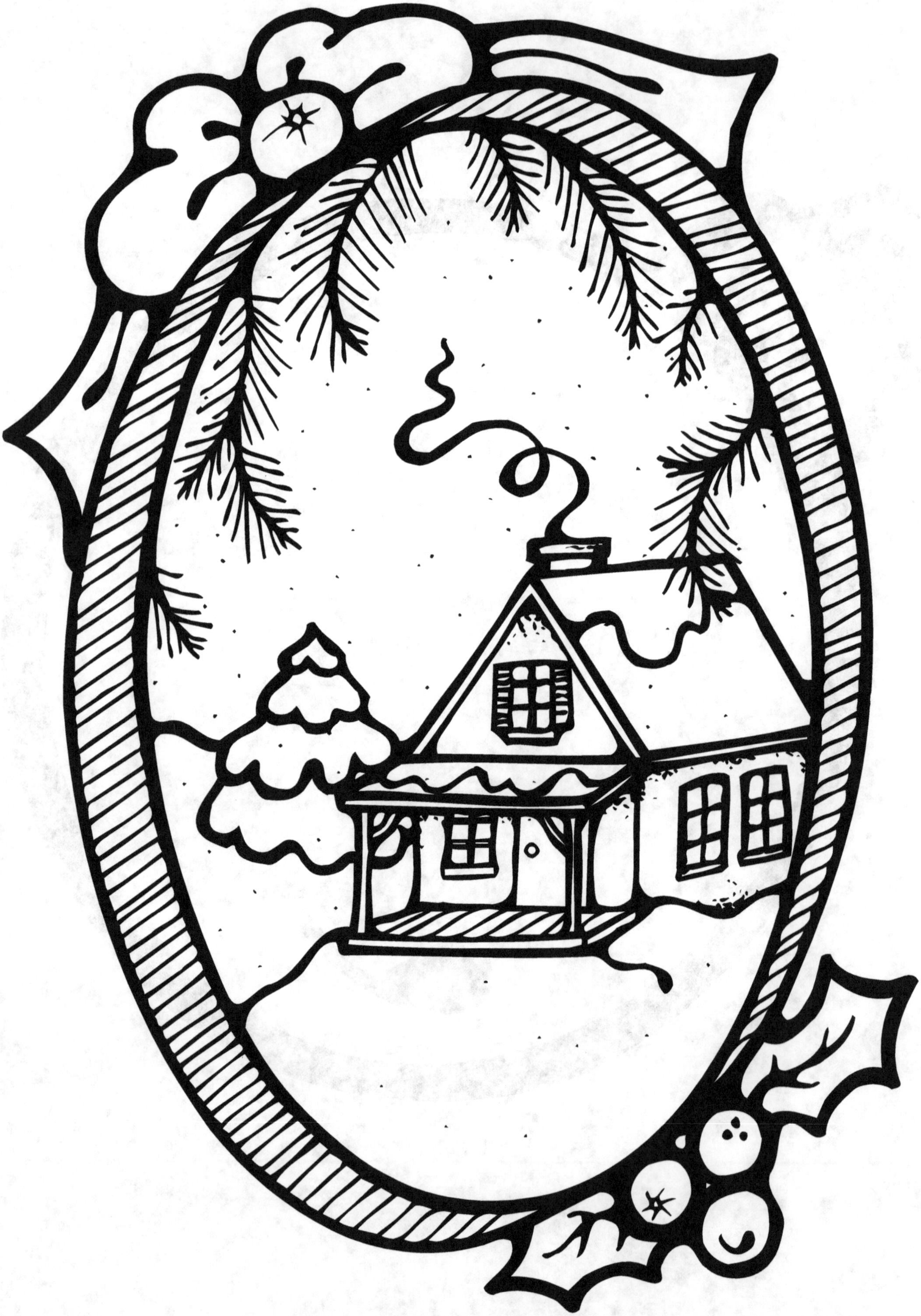

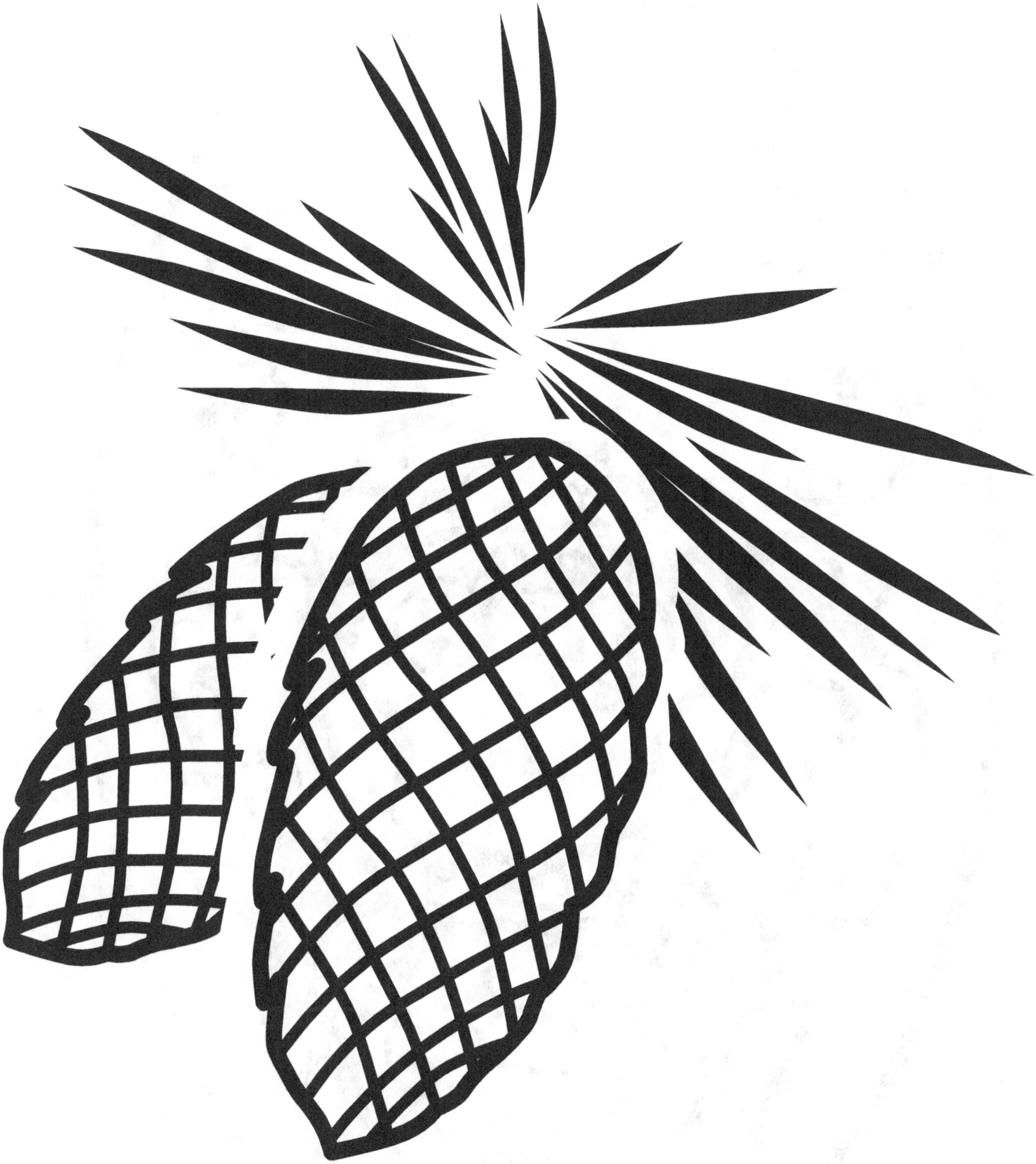

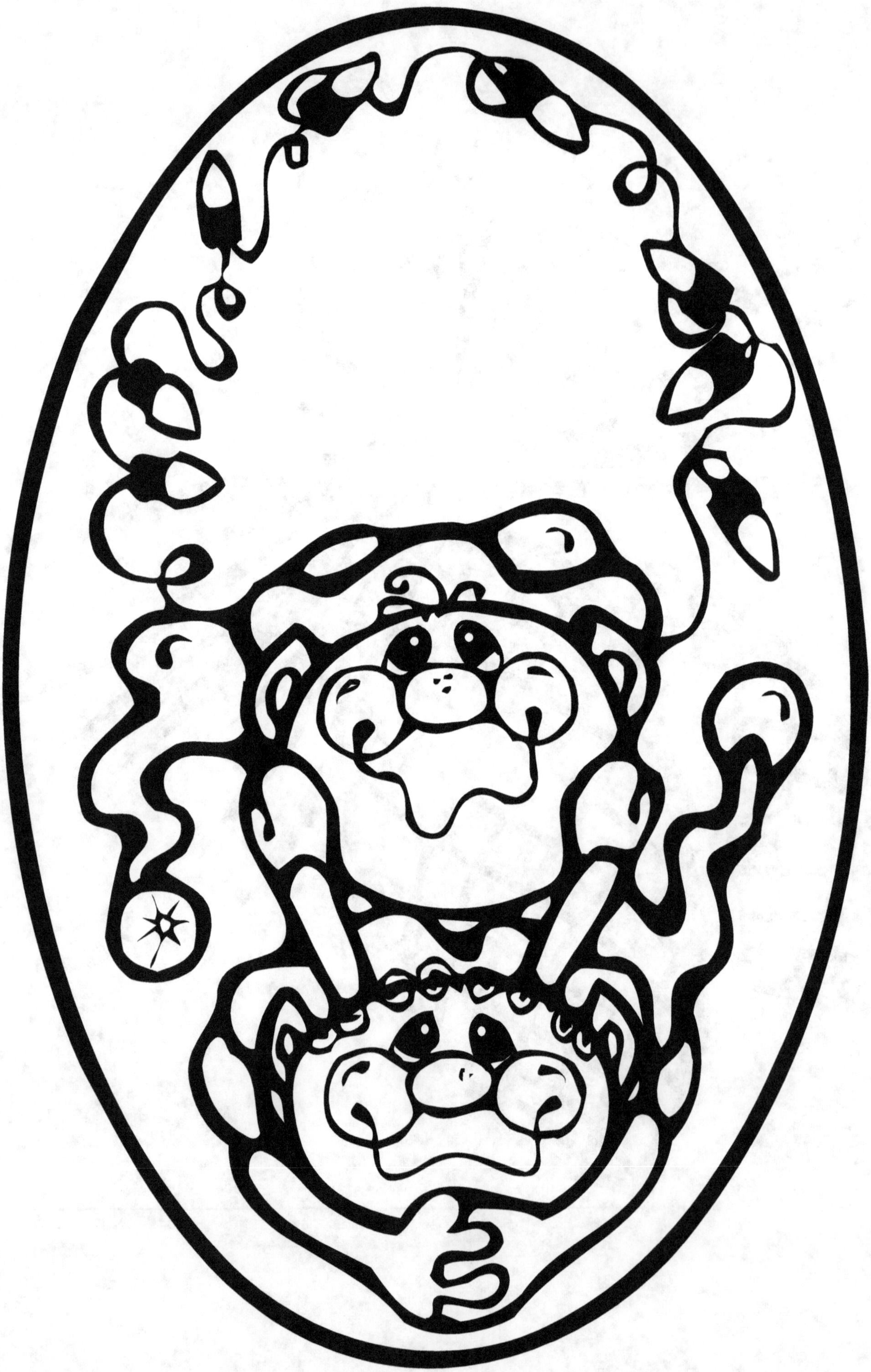

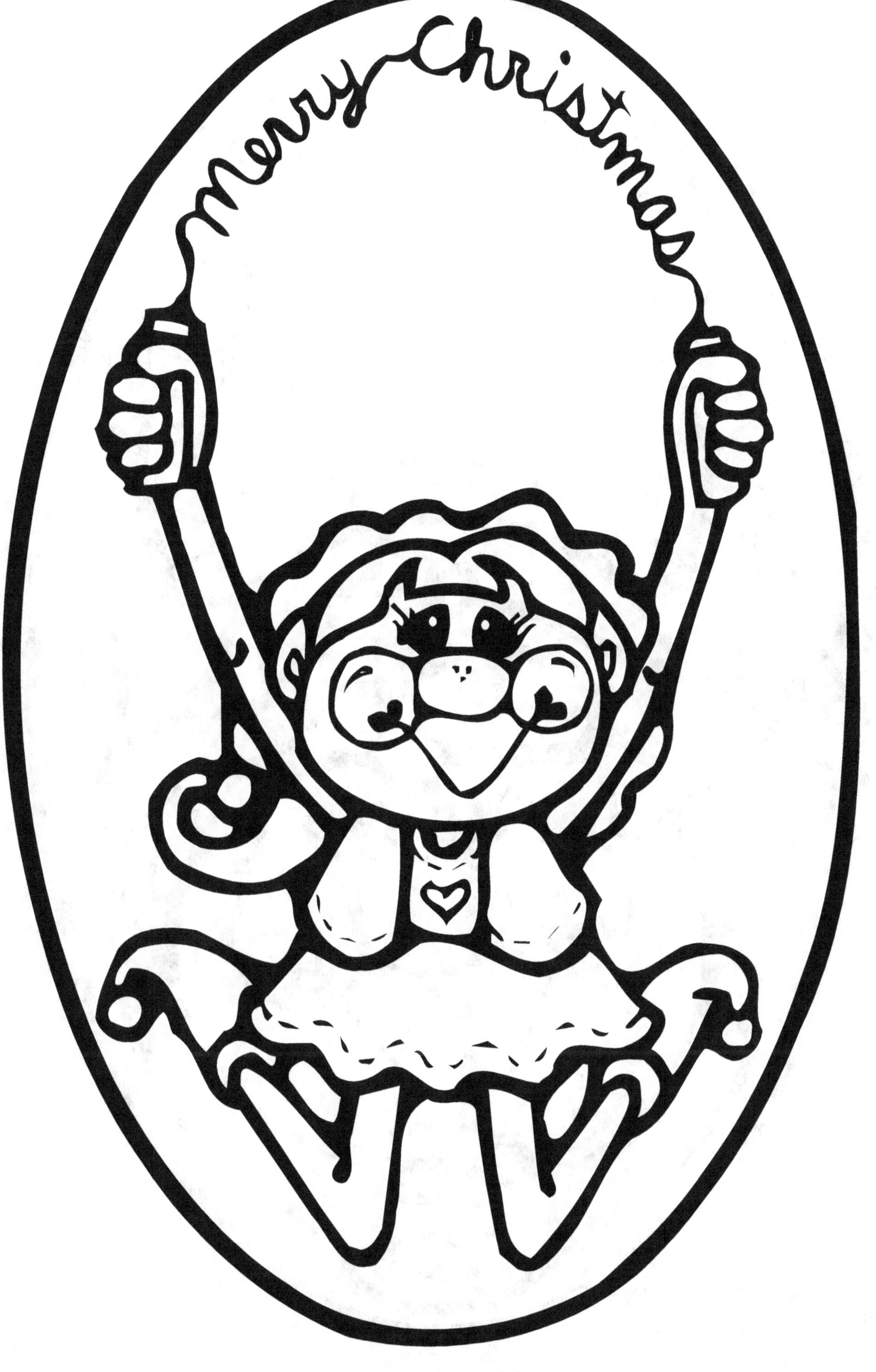
Merry Christmas

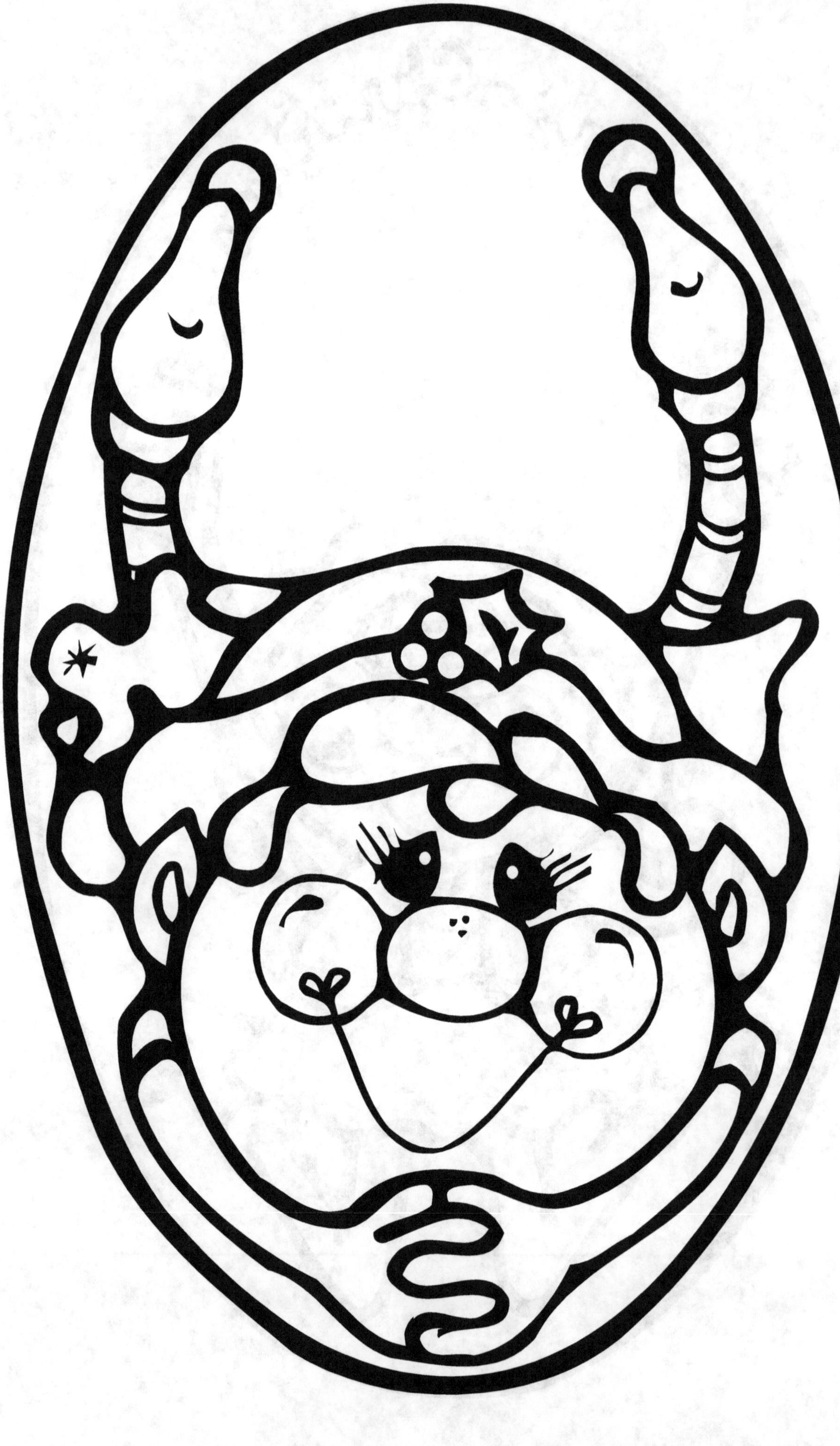

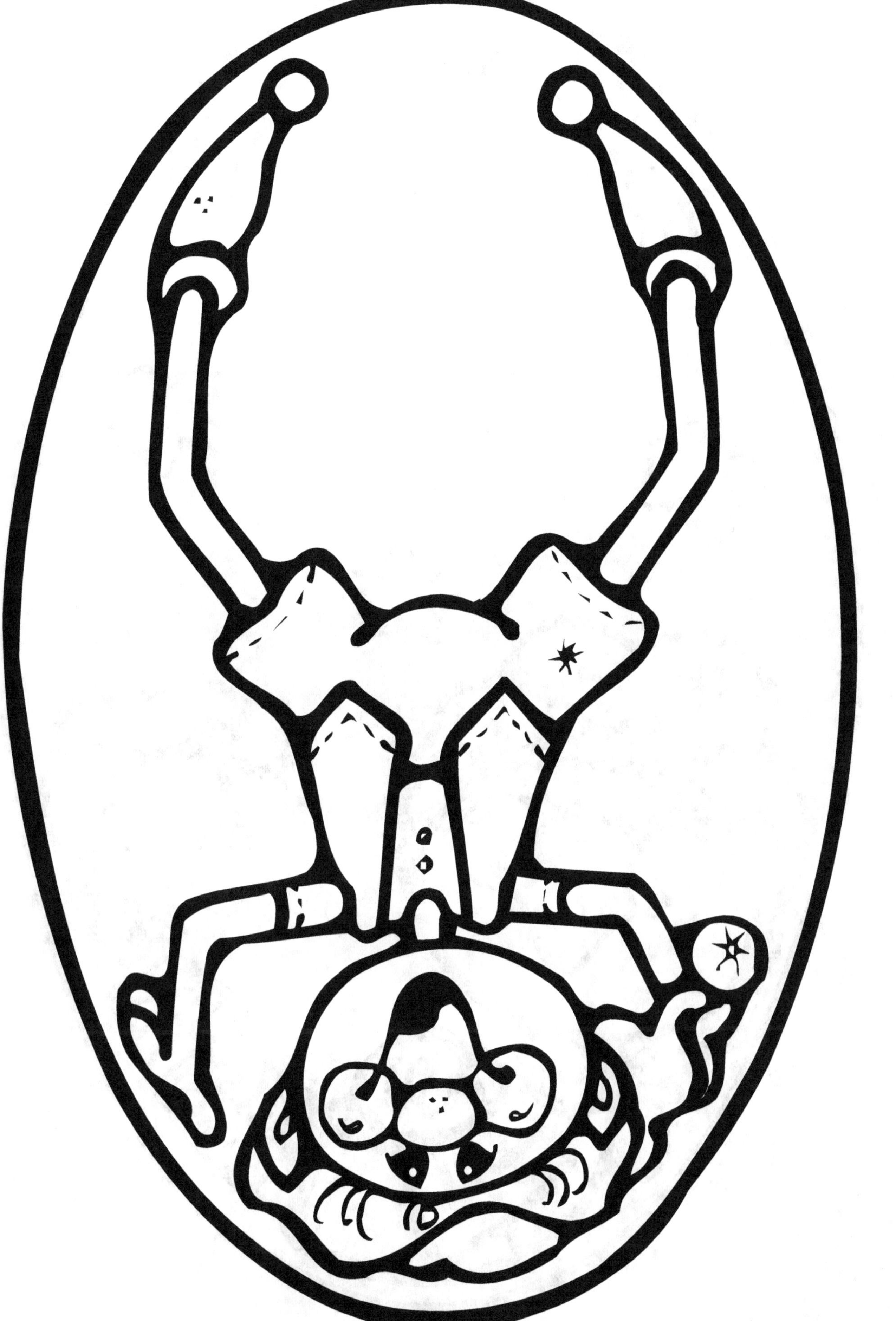

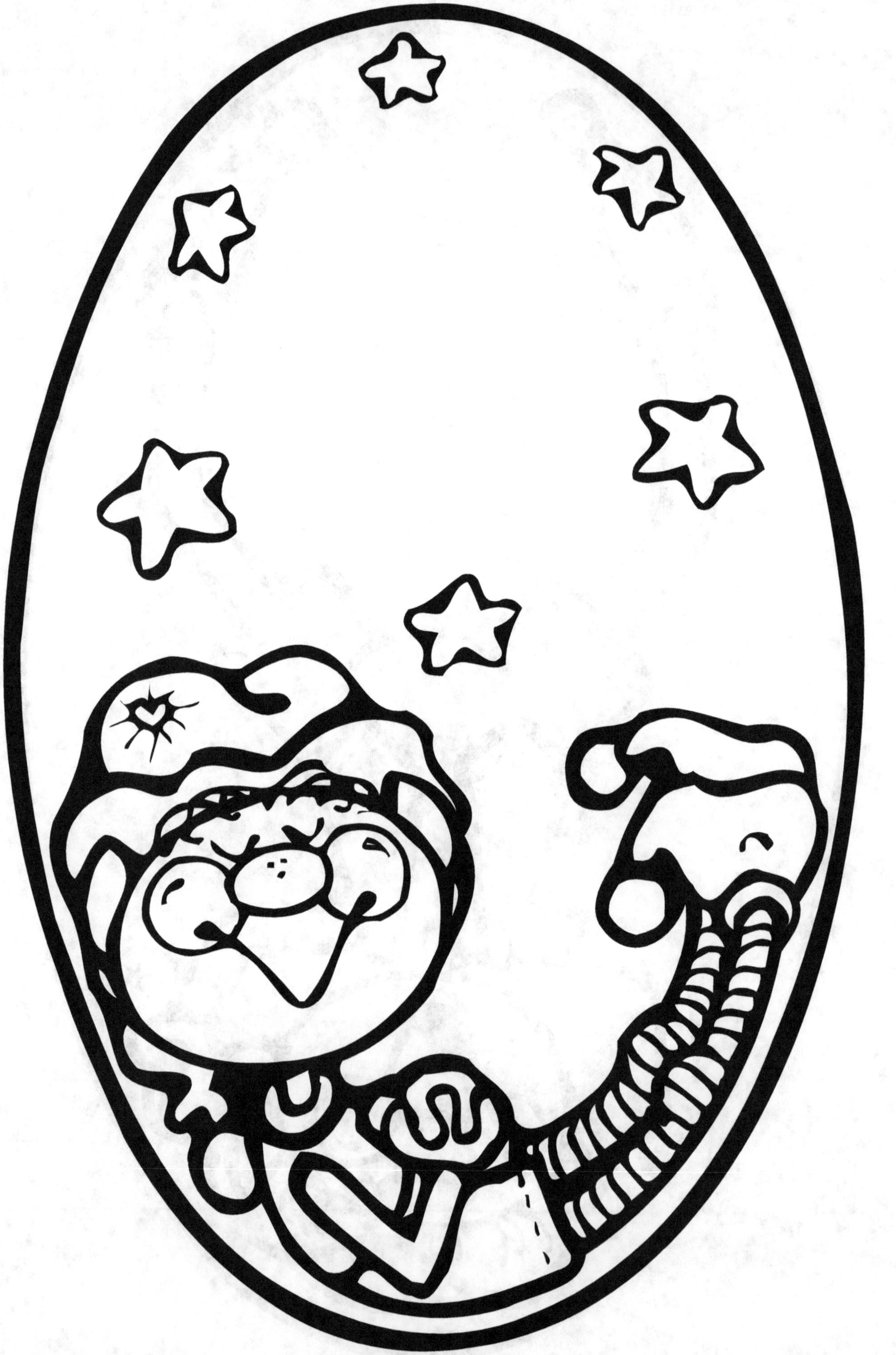

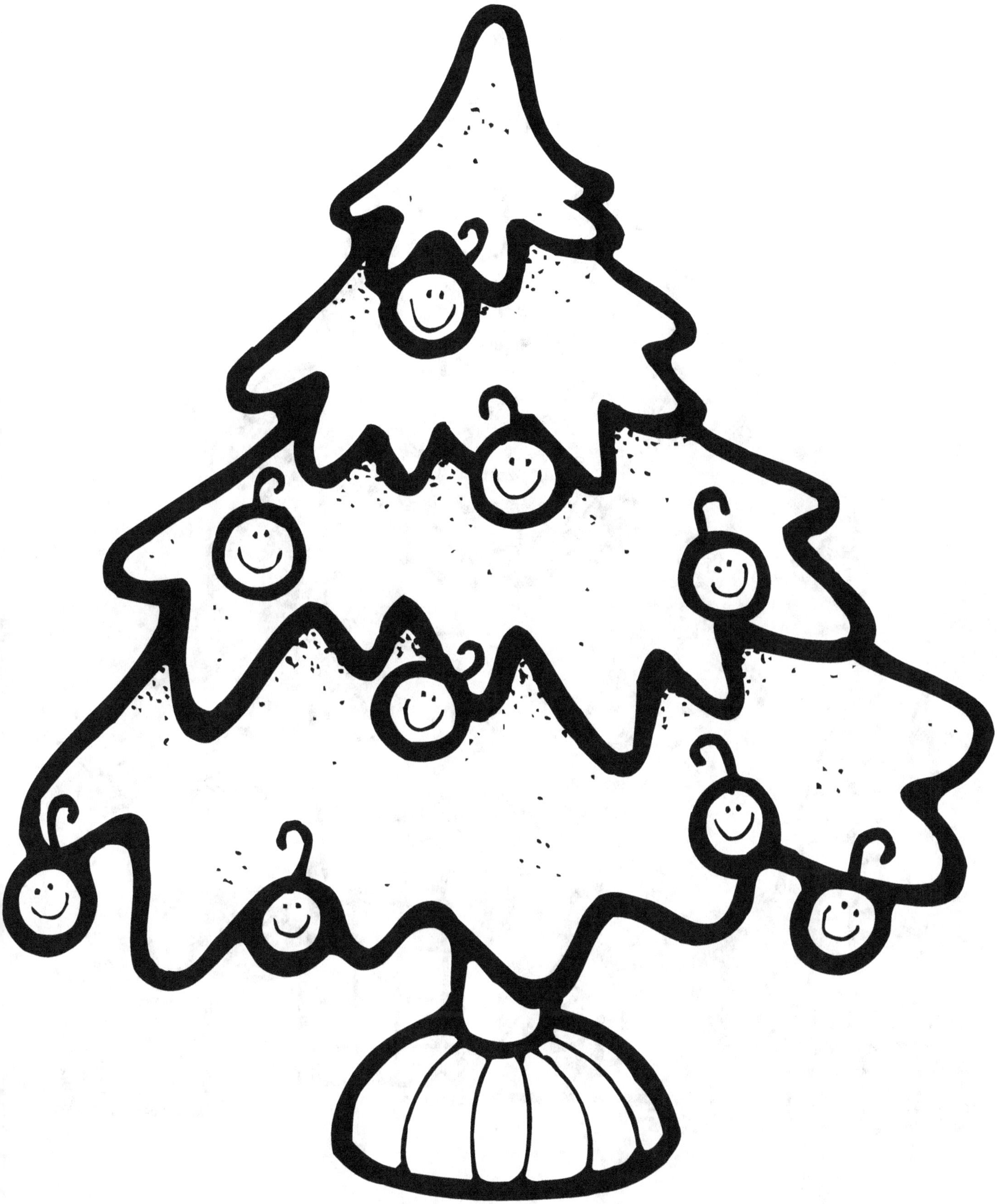

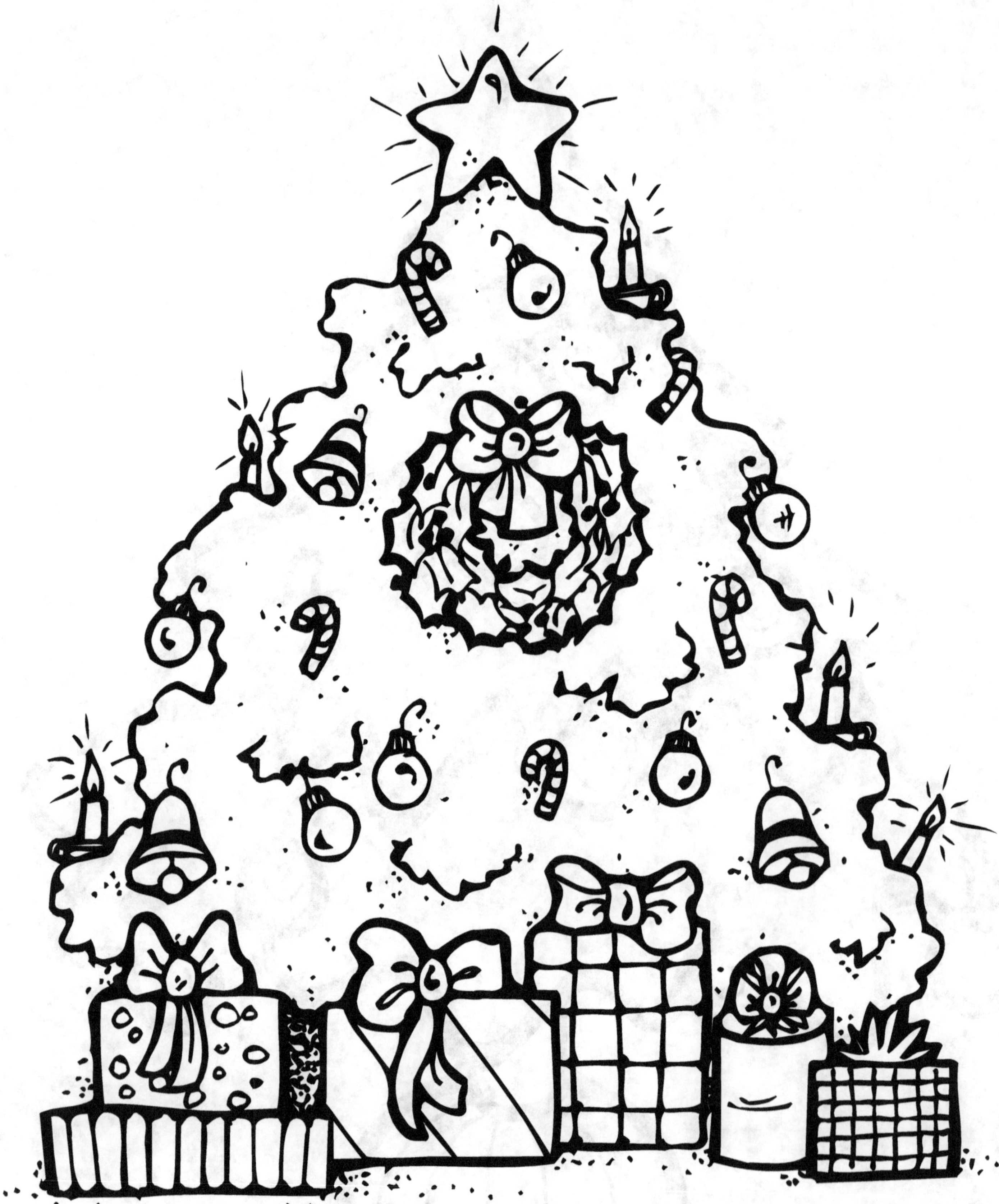

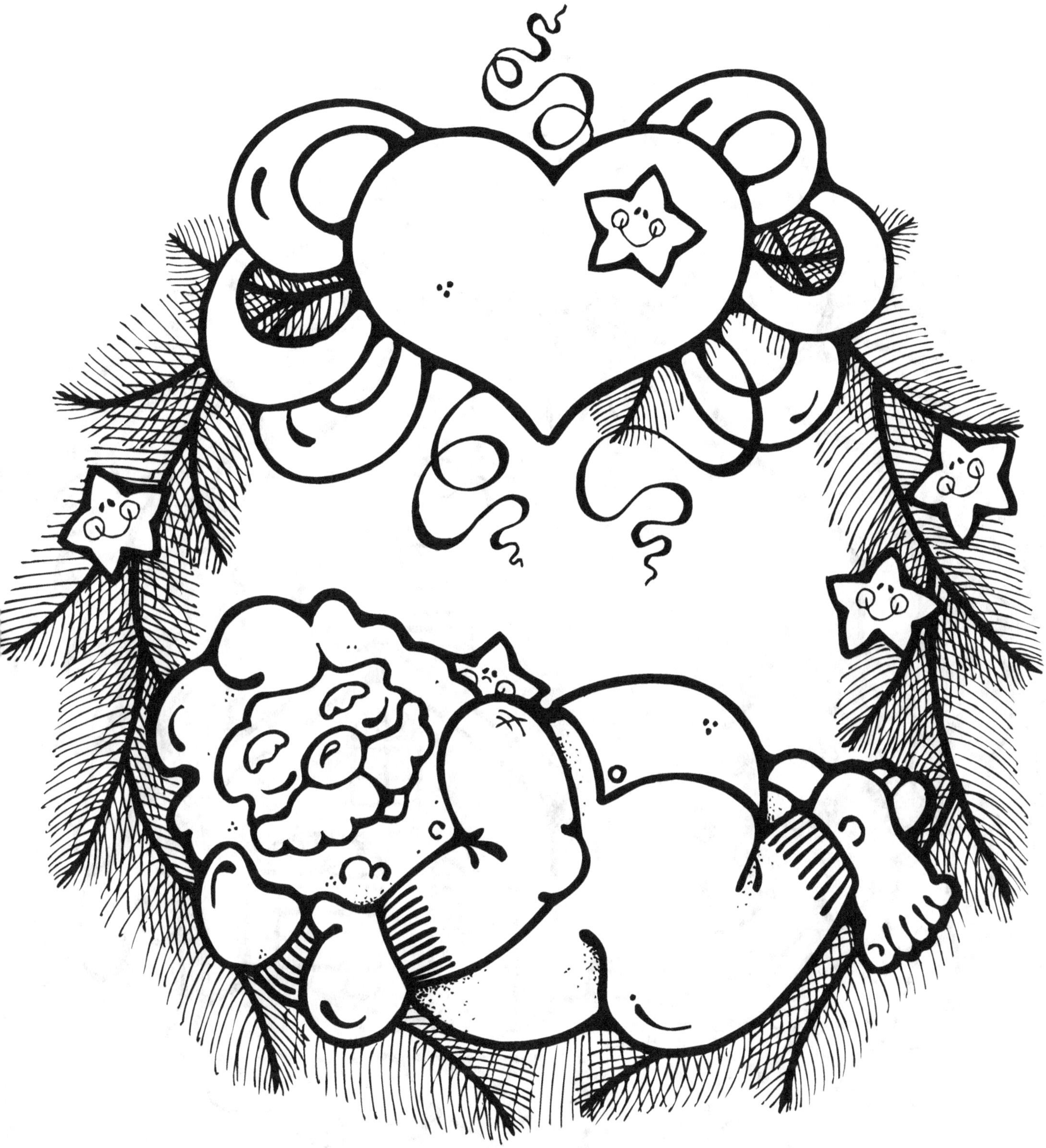

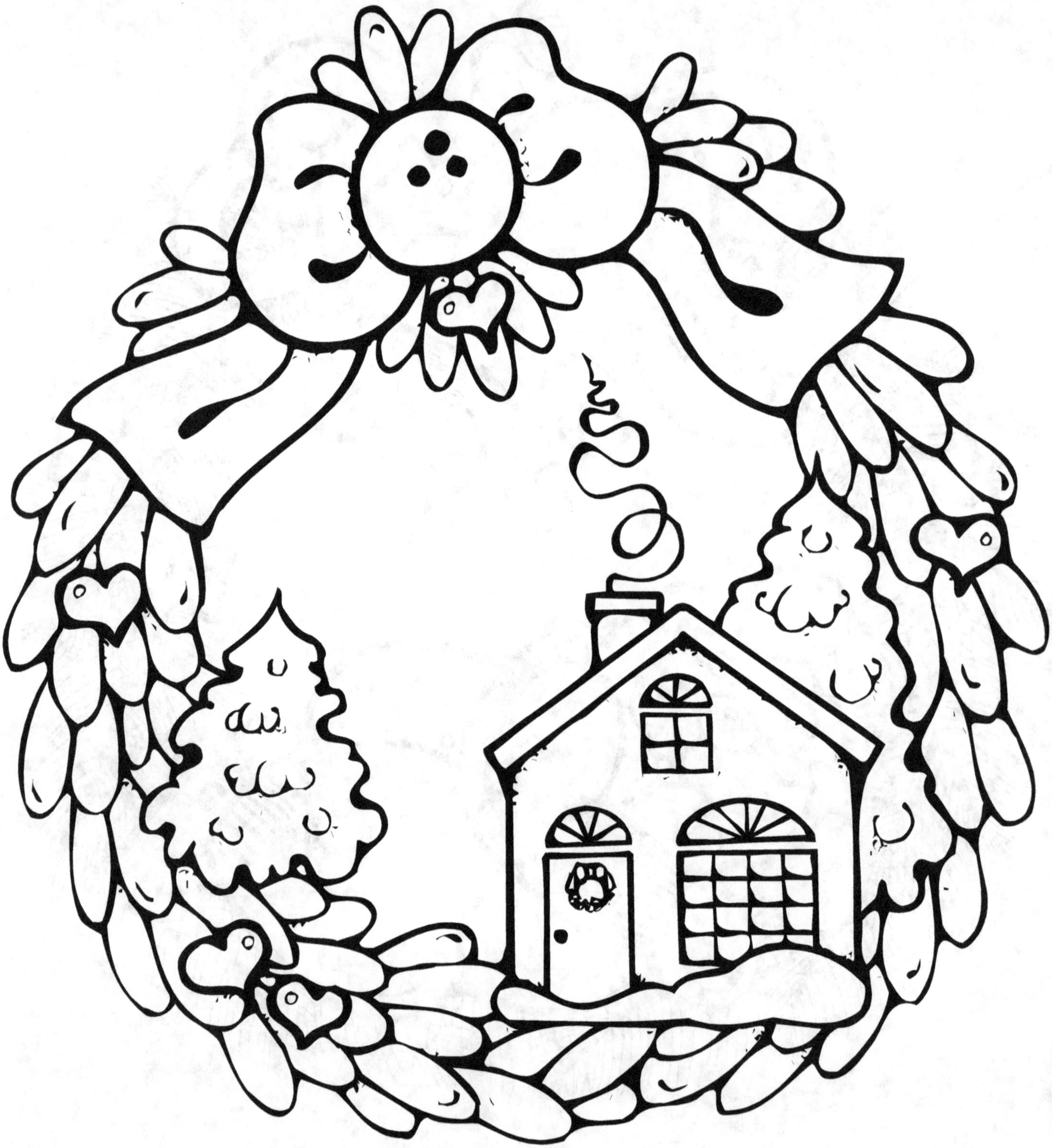

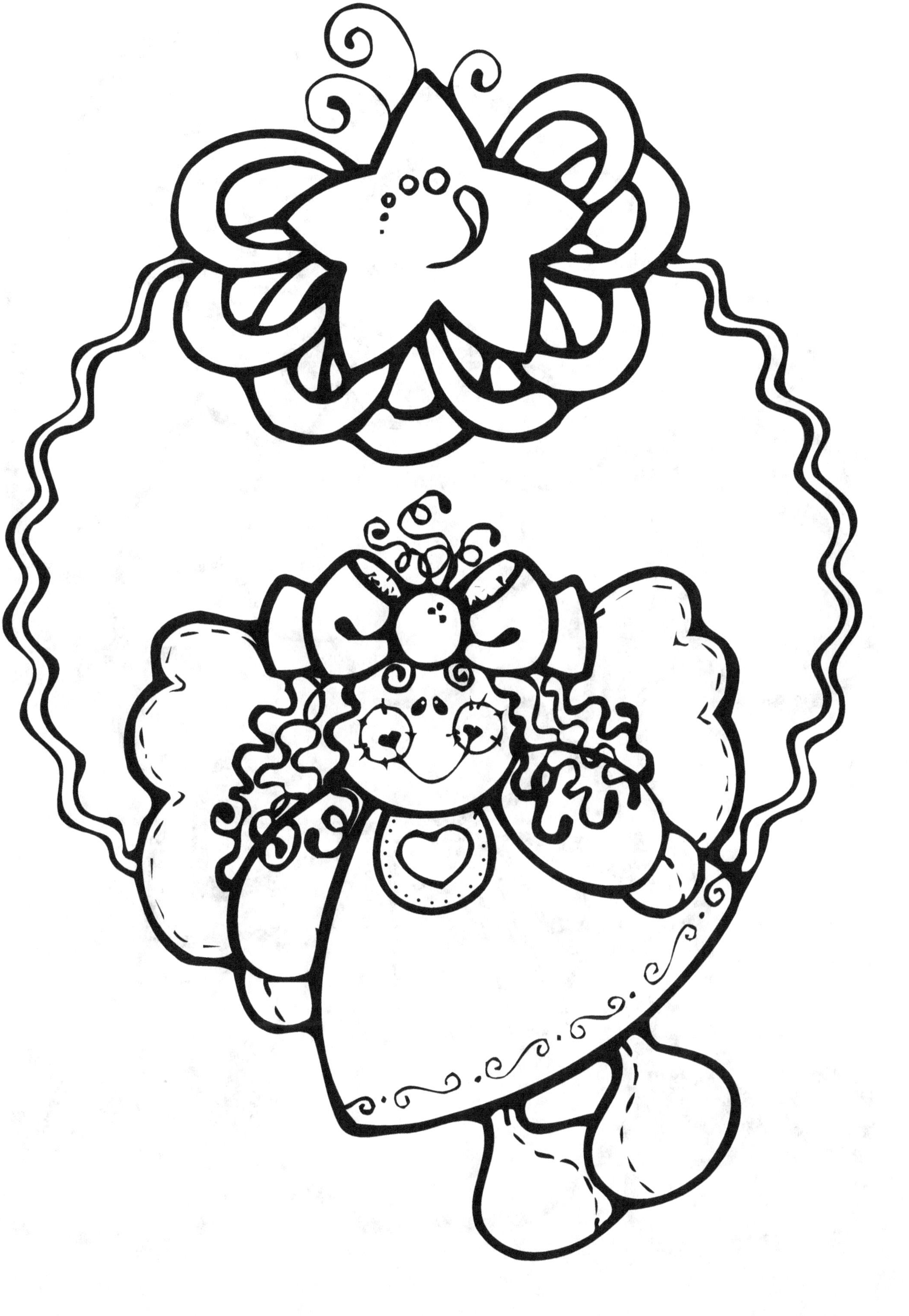

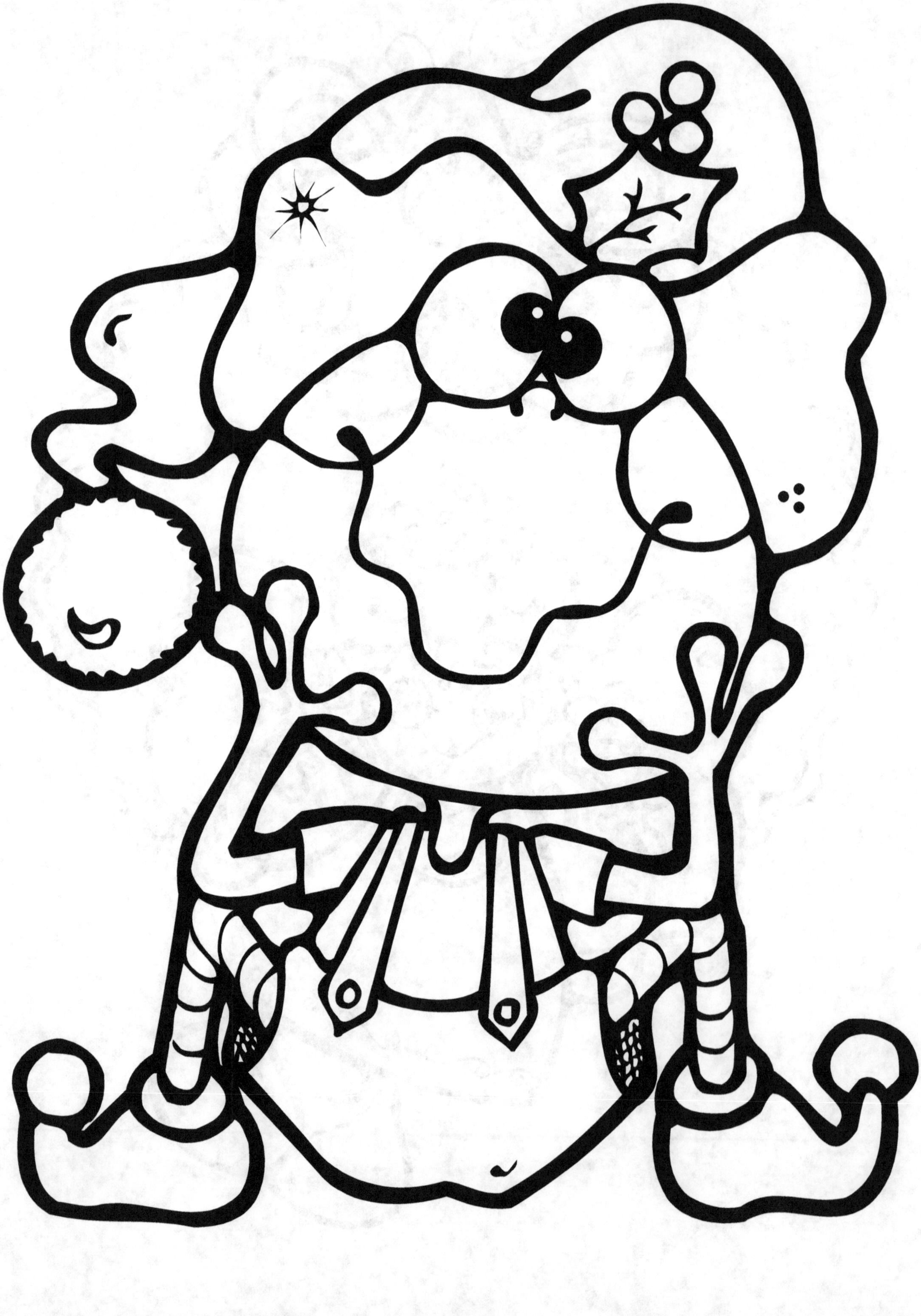

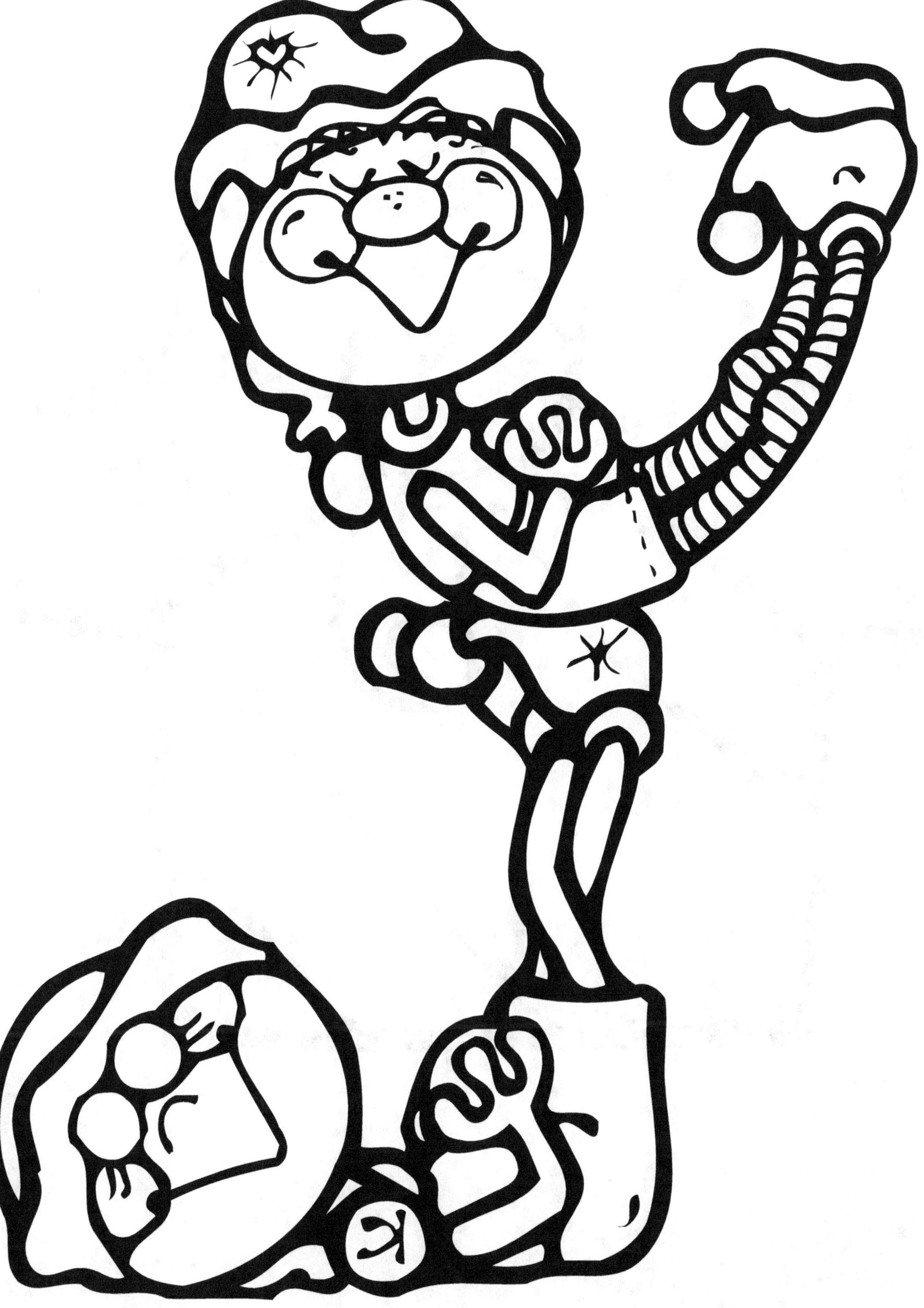

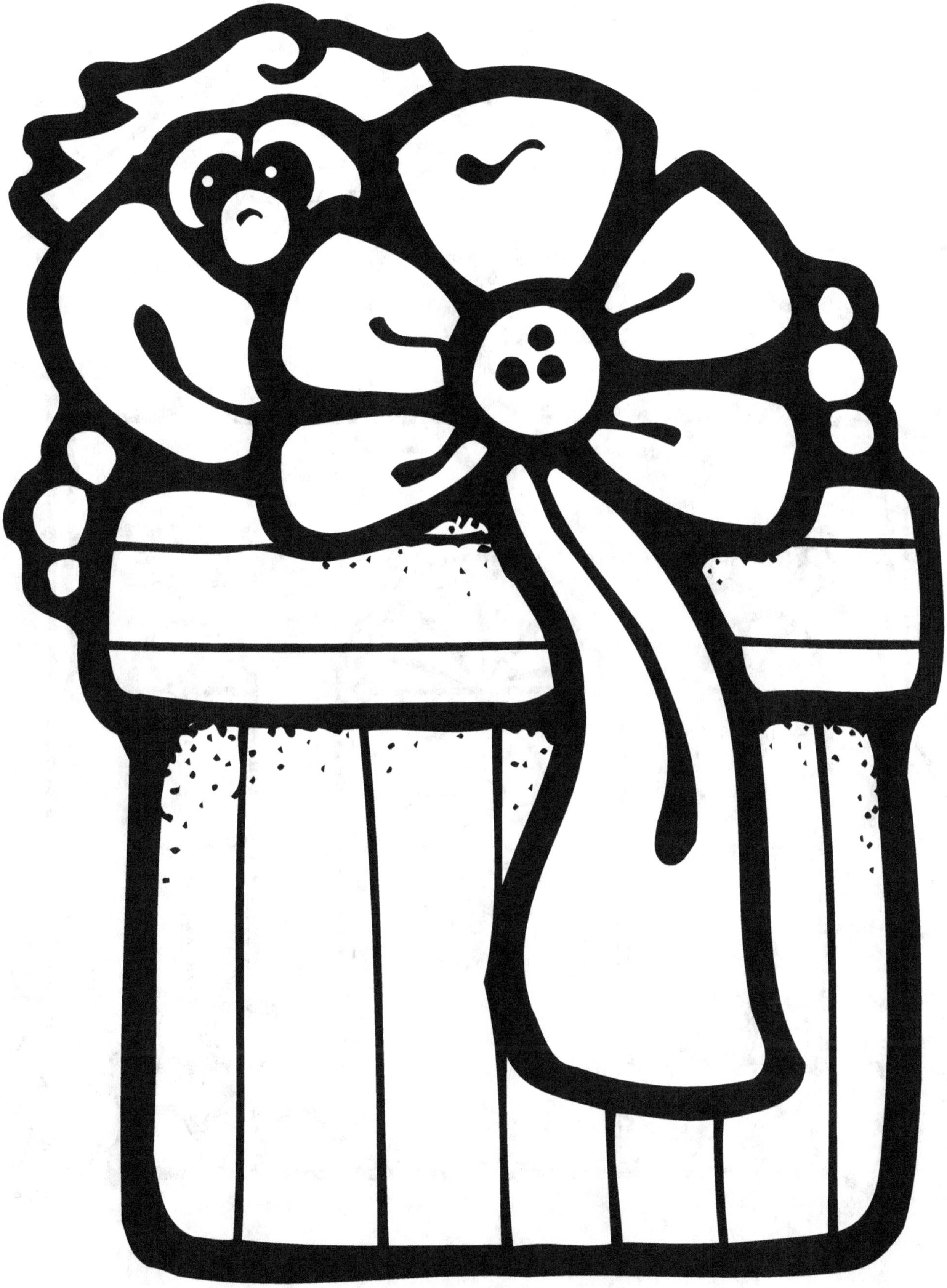

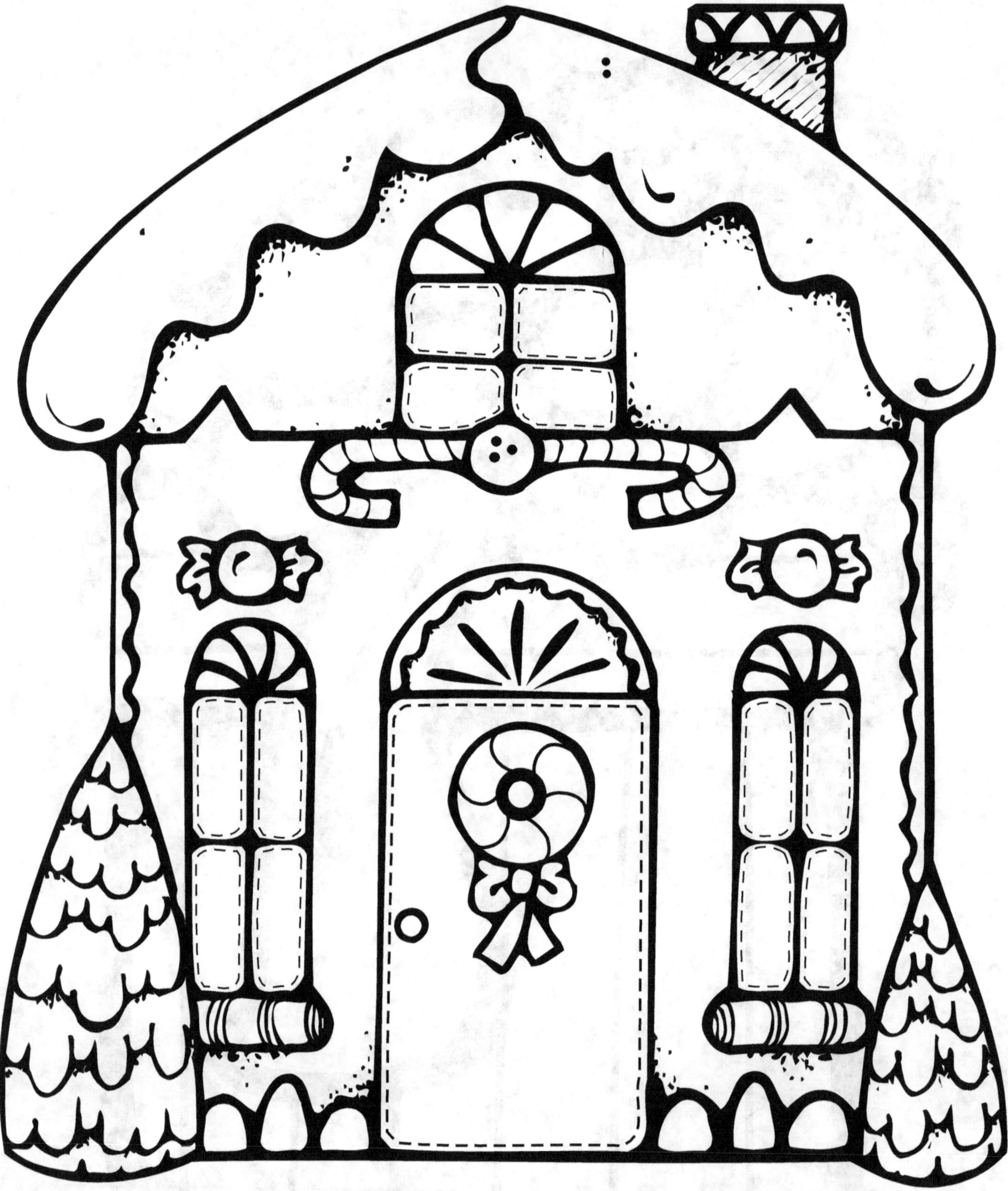

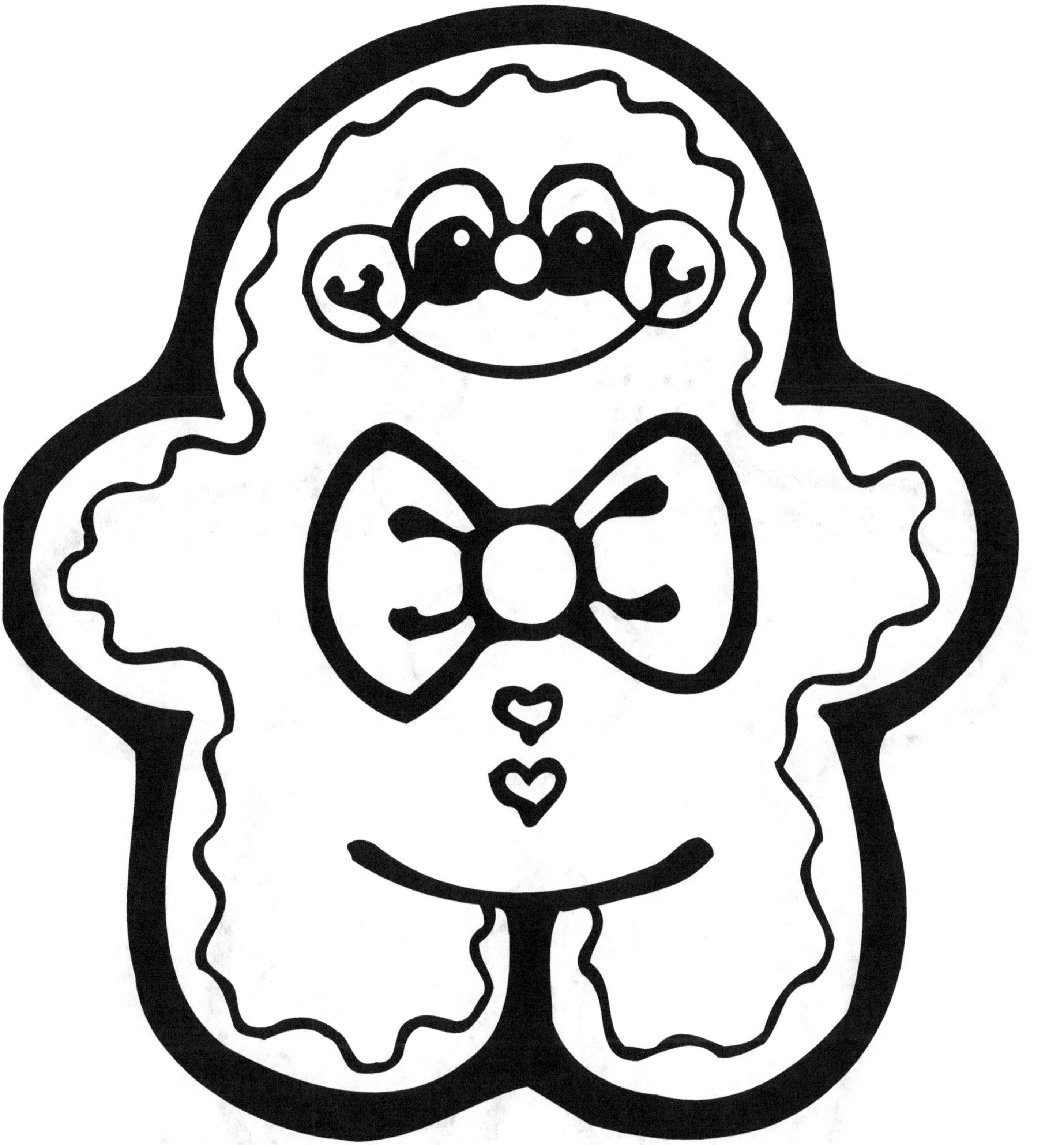

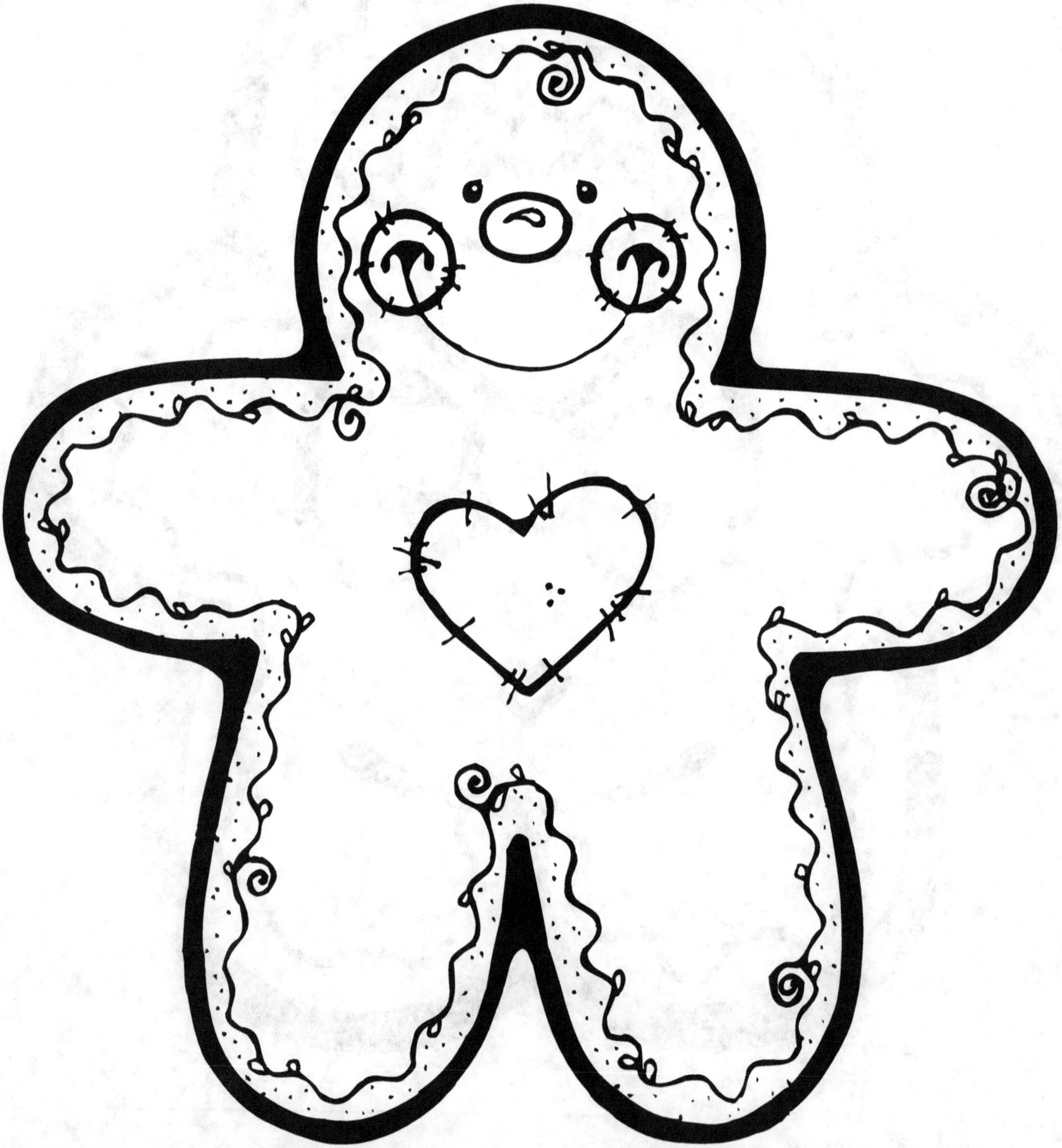

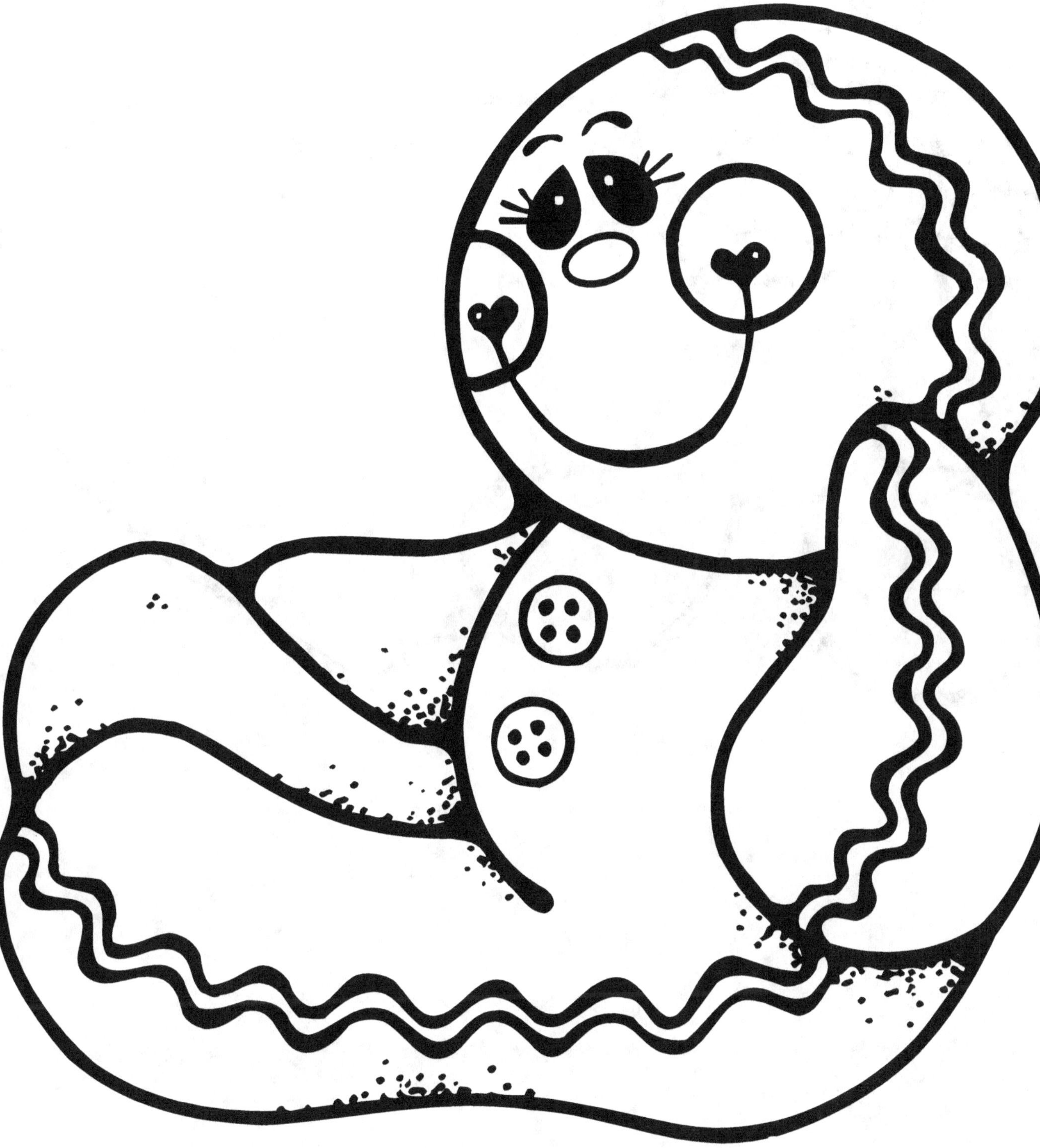

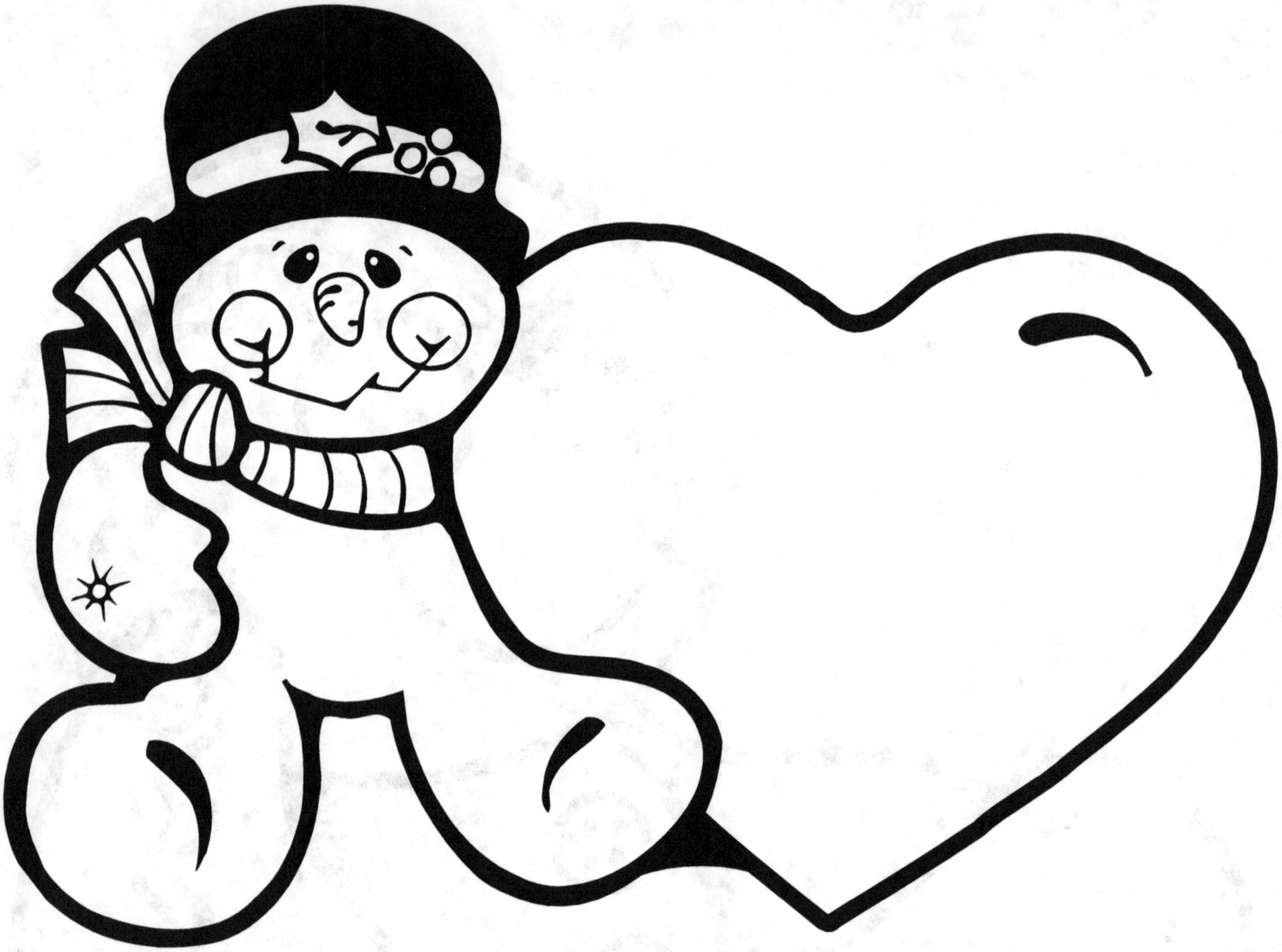

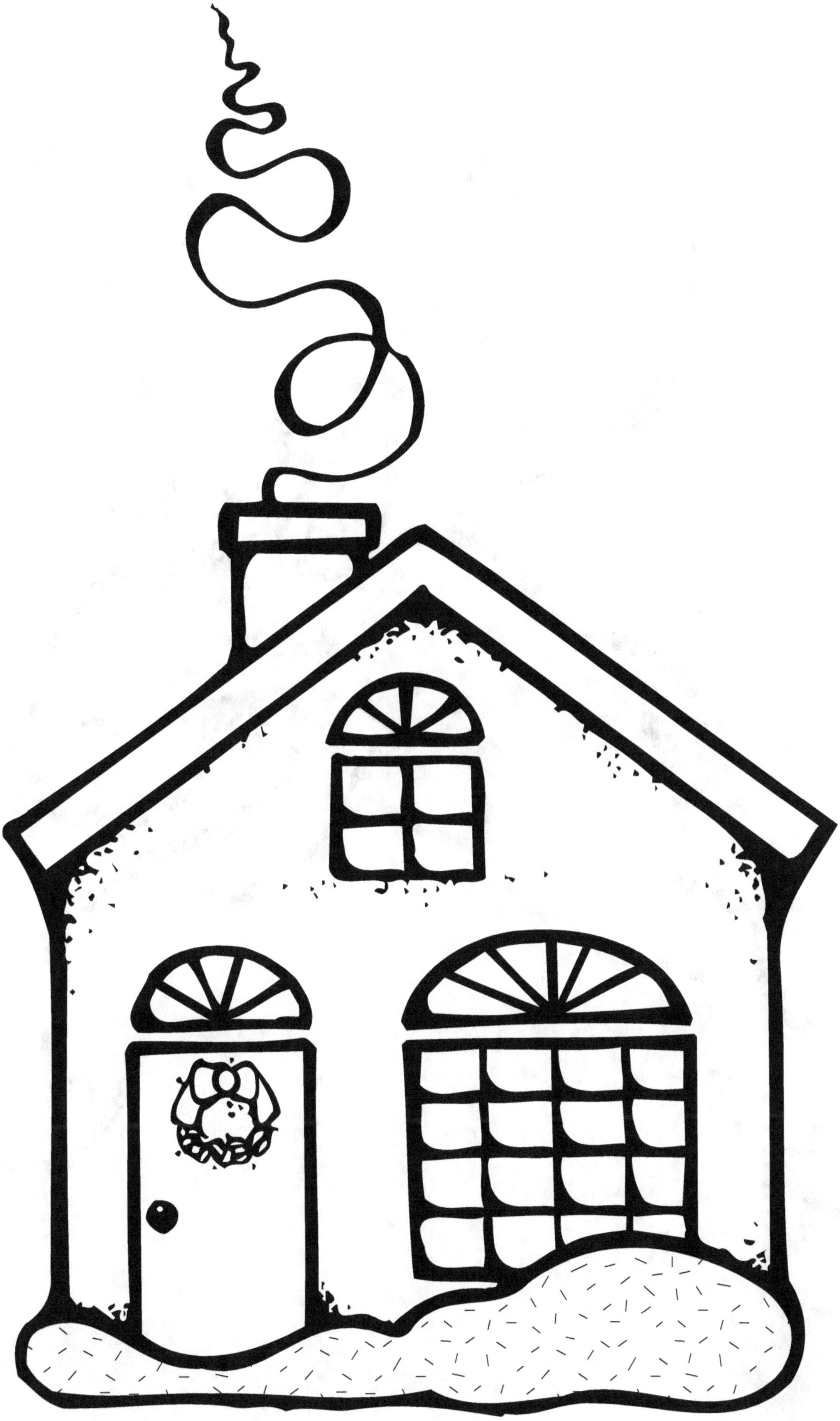

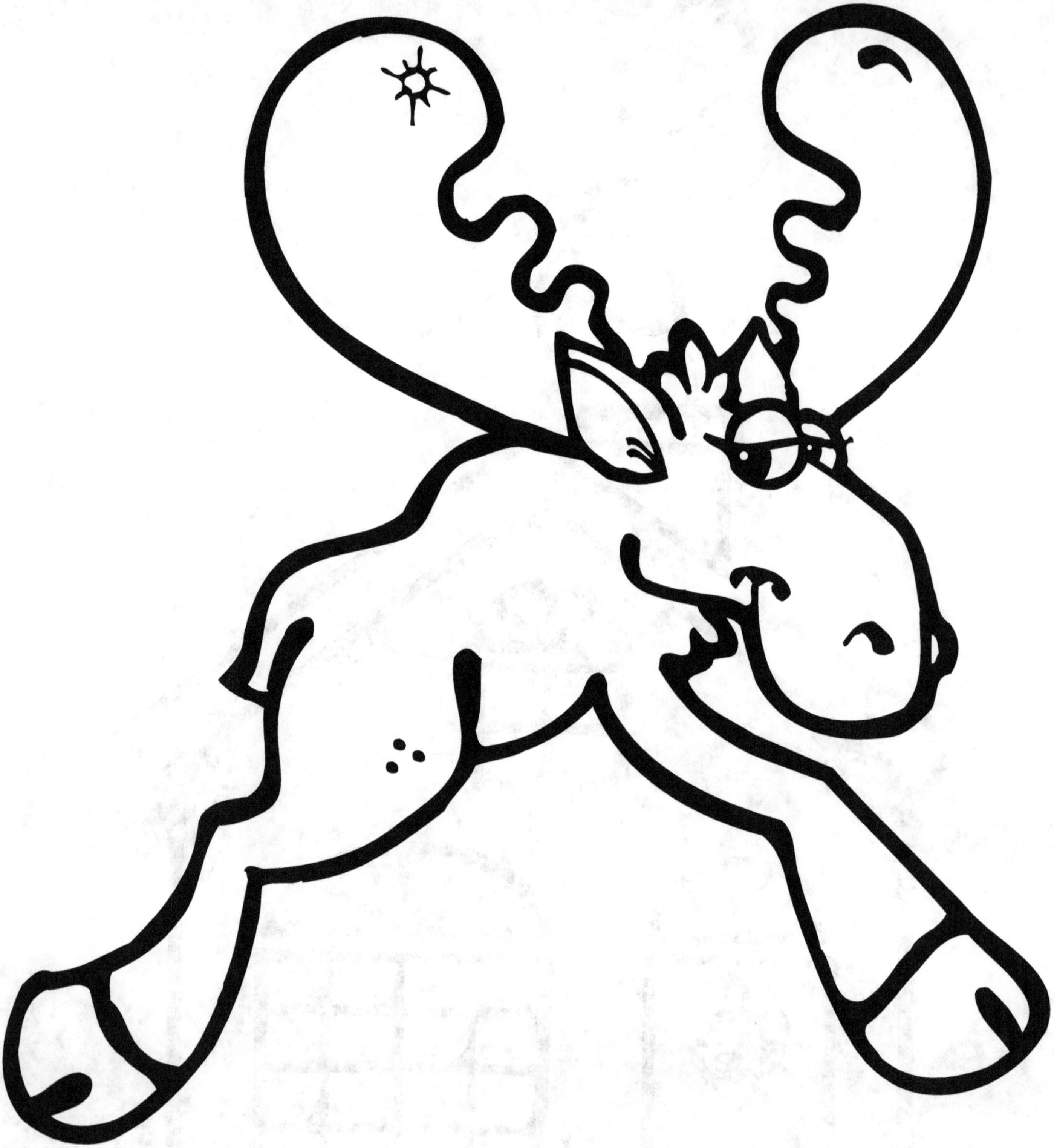

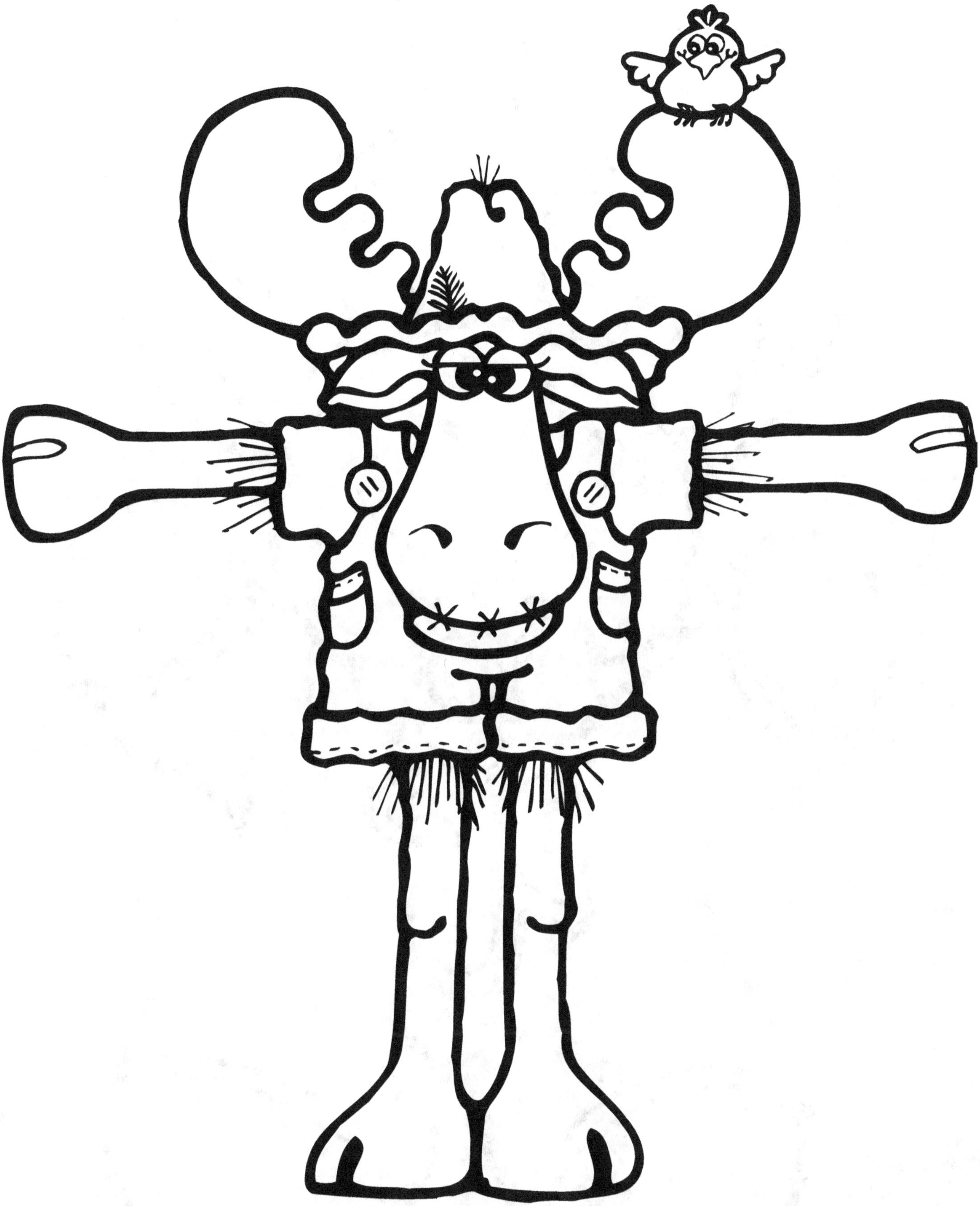

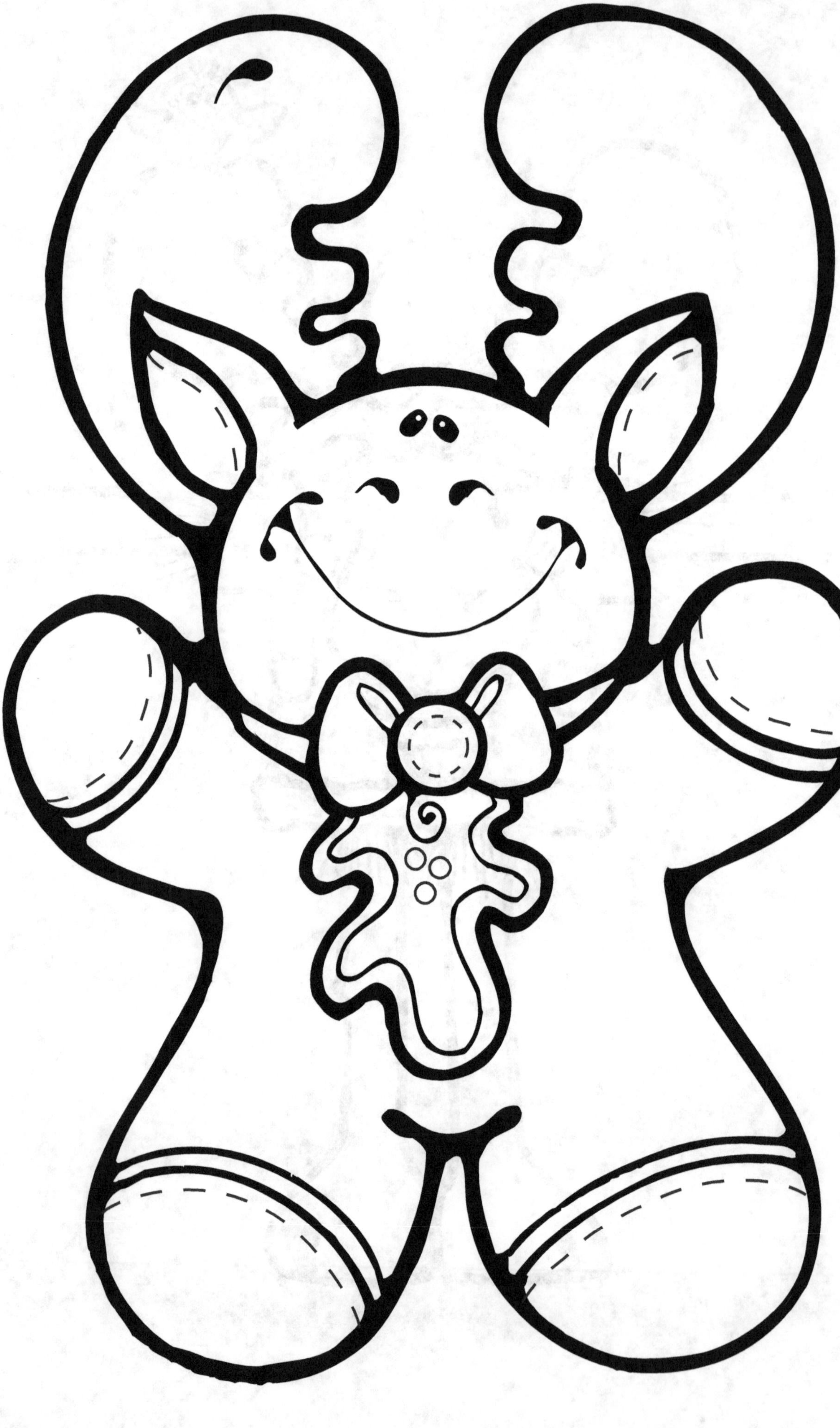

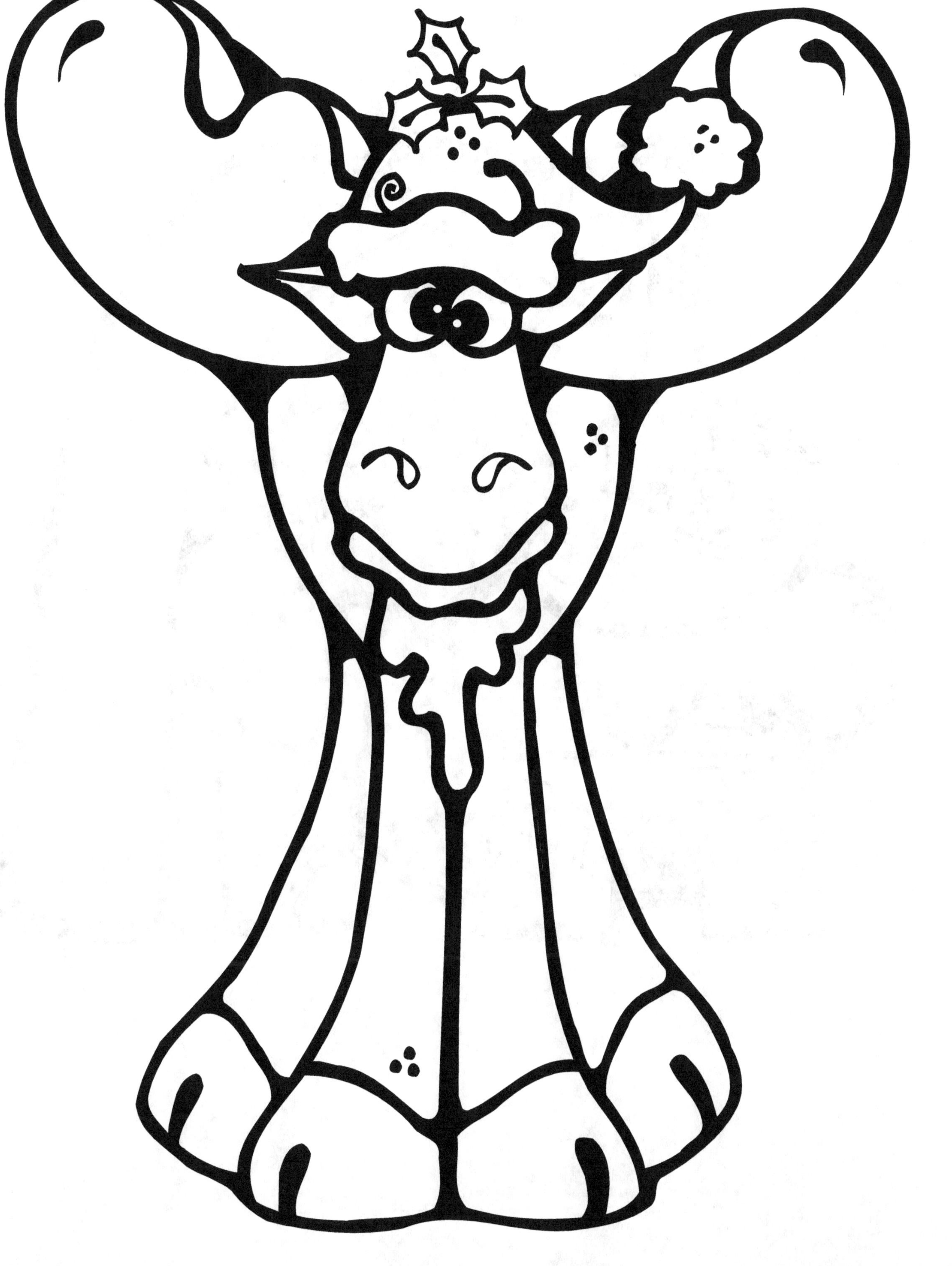

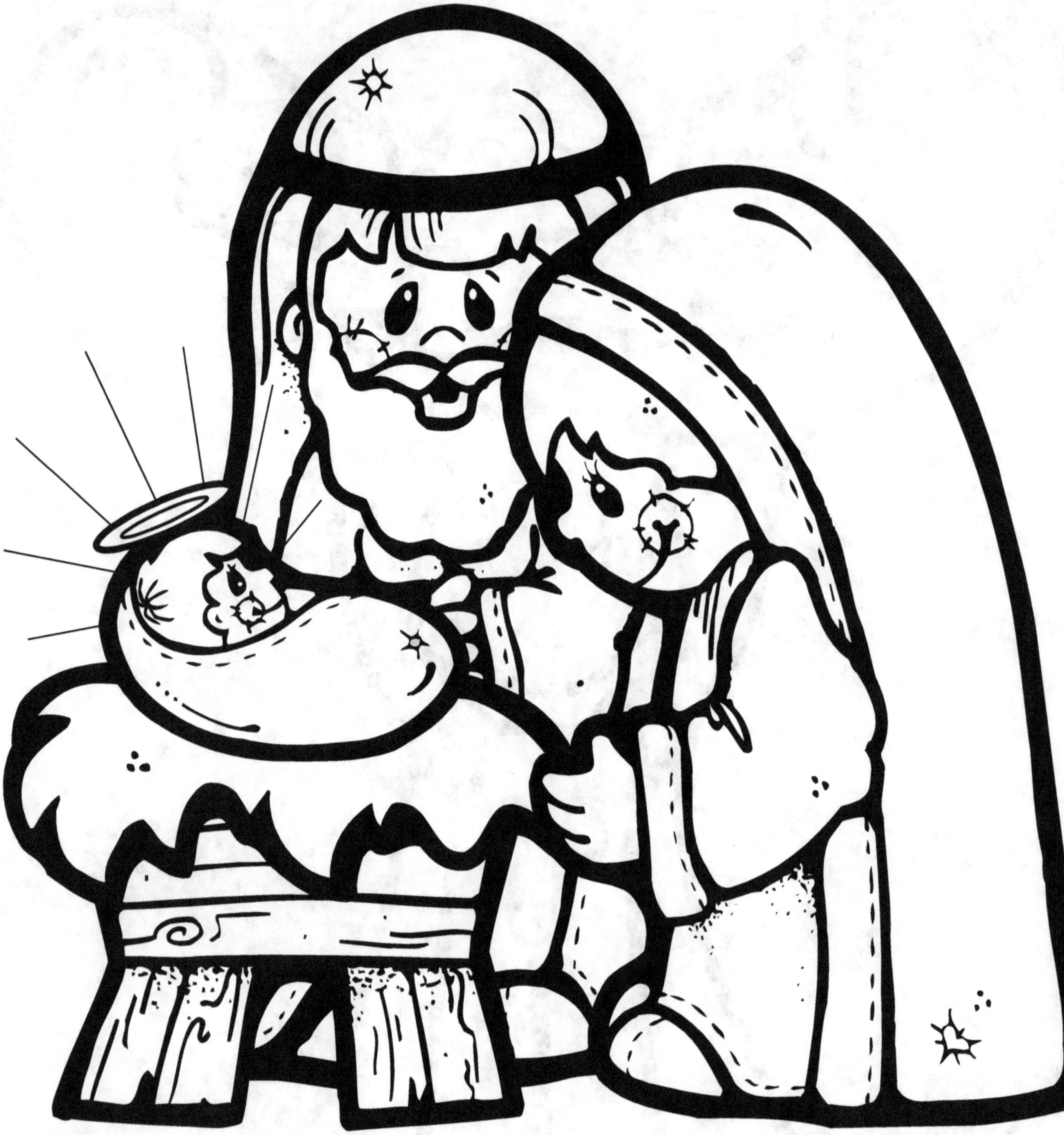

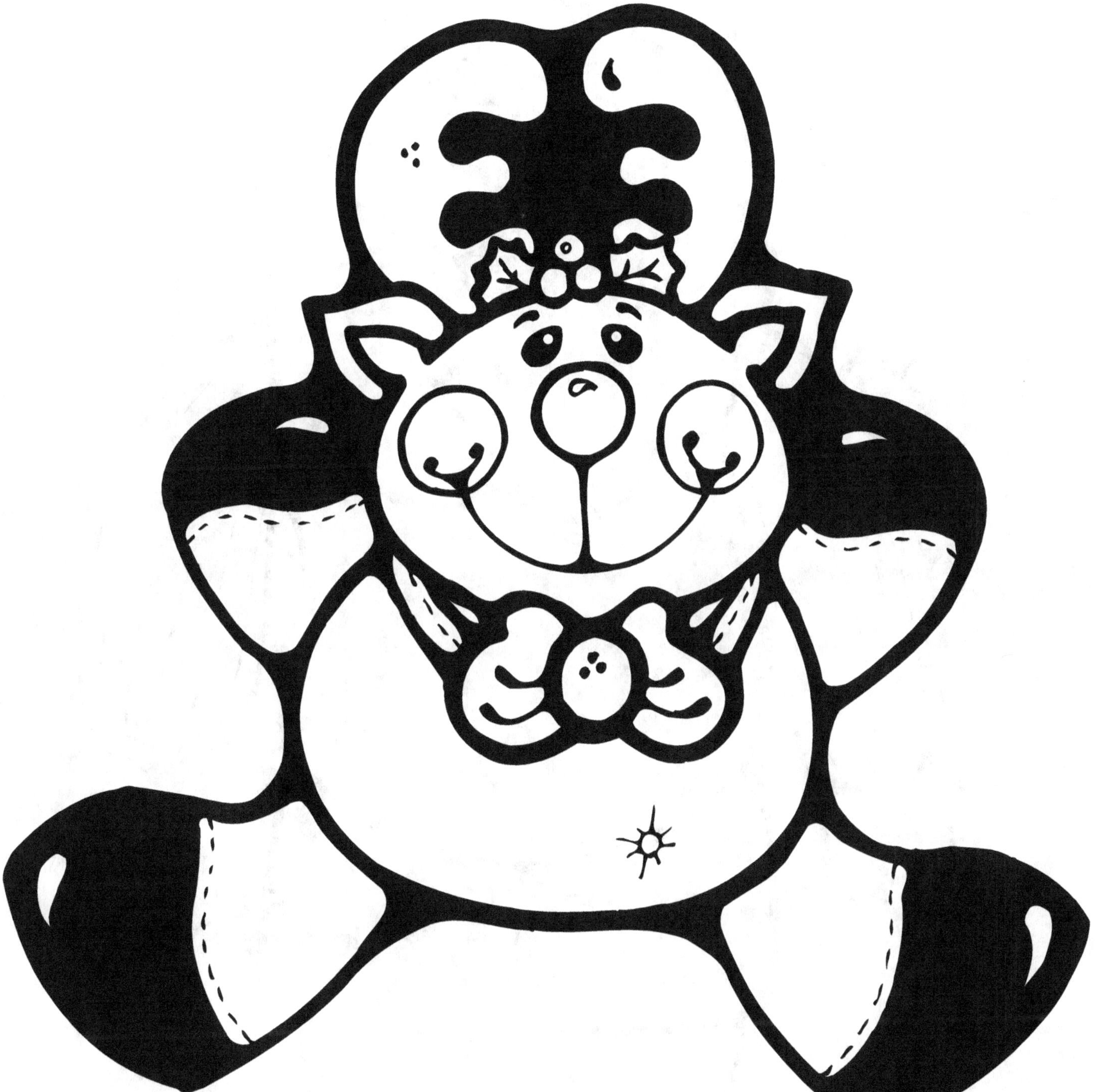

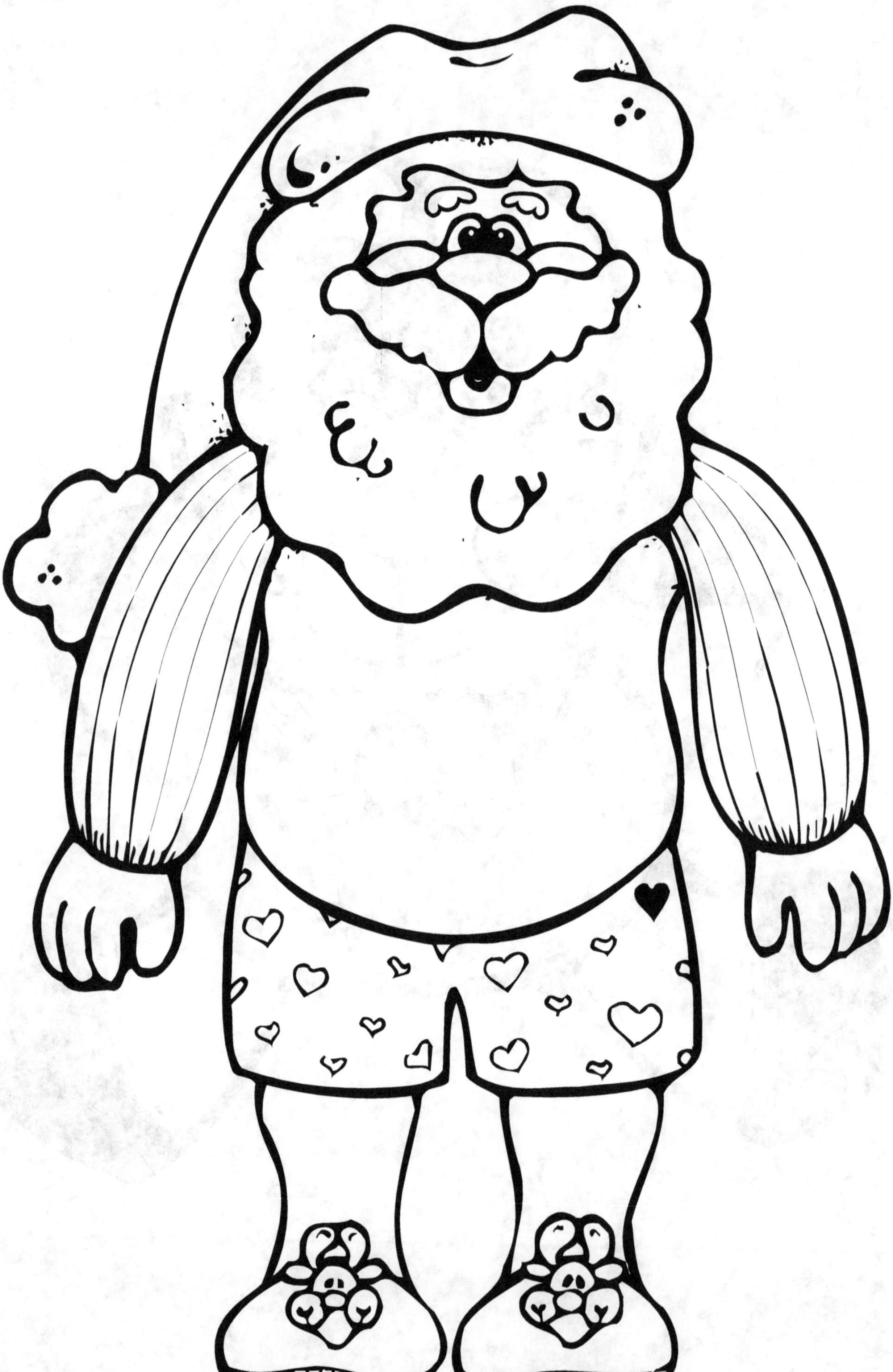

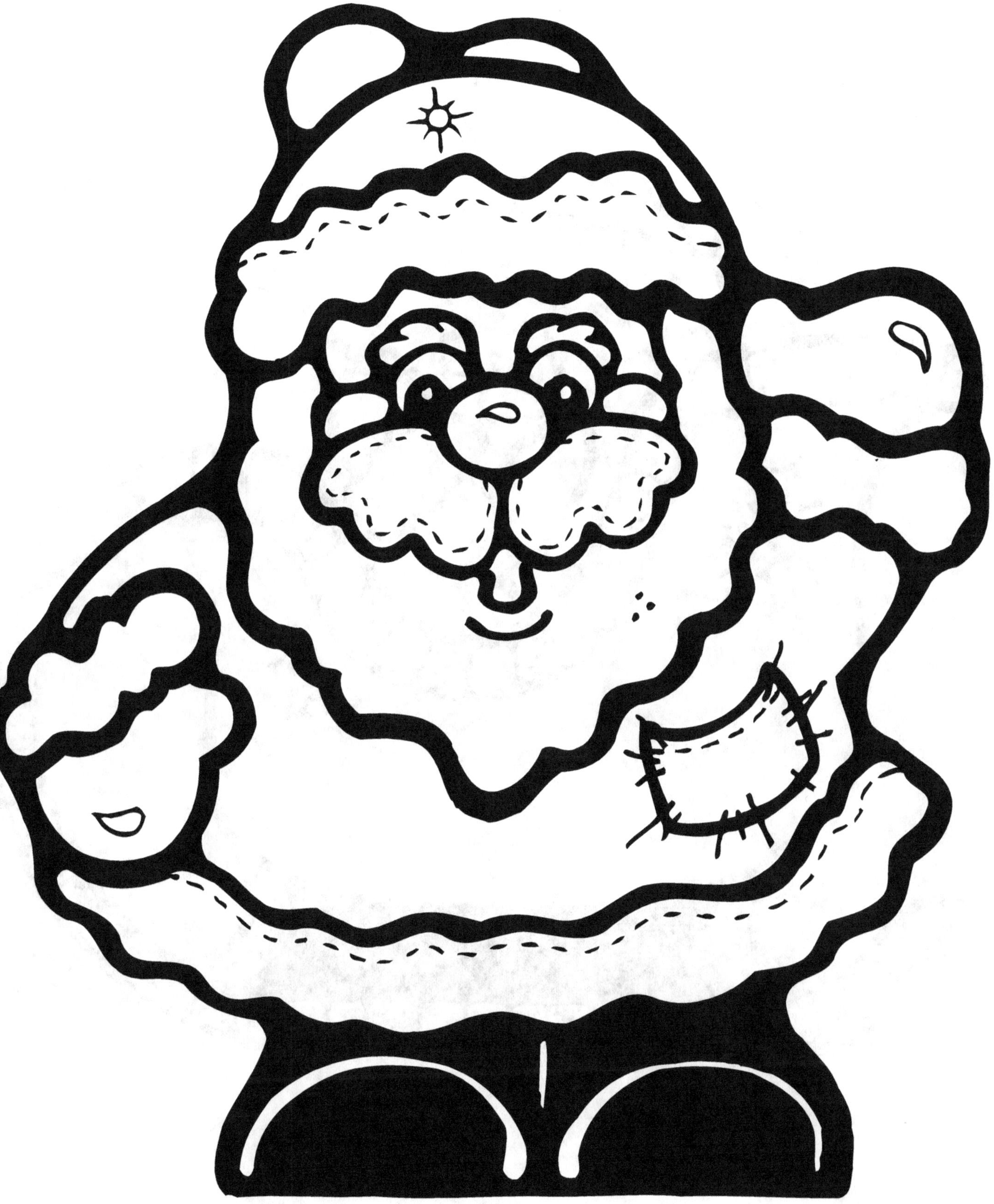

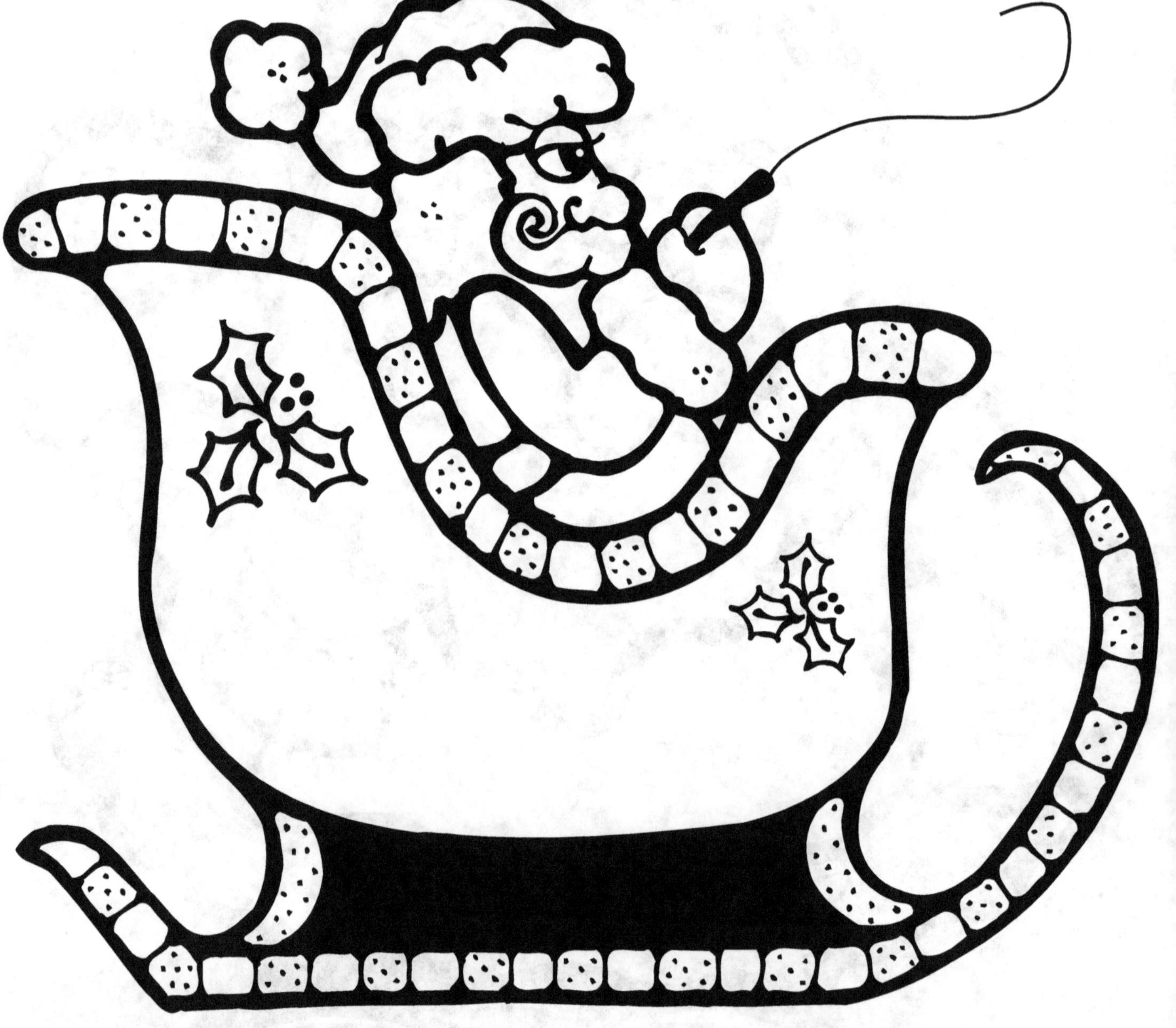

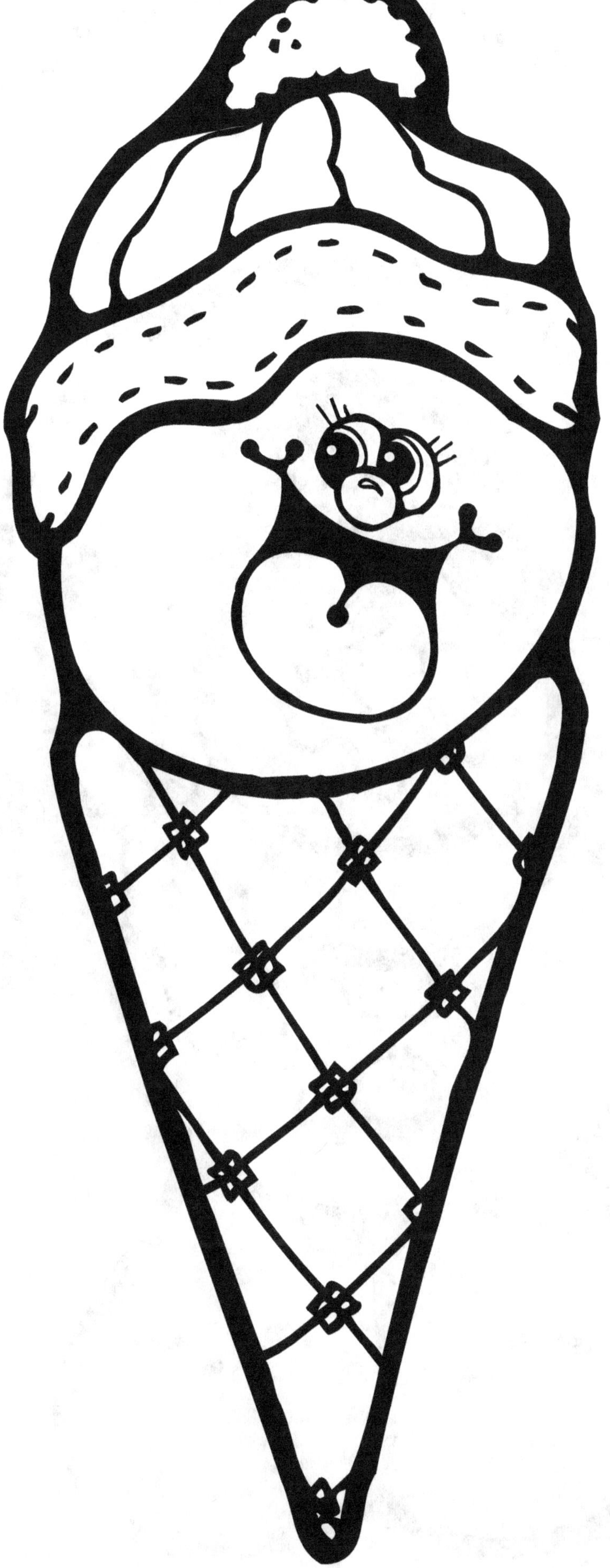

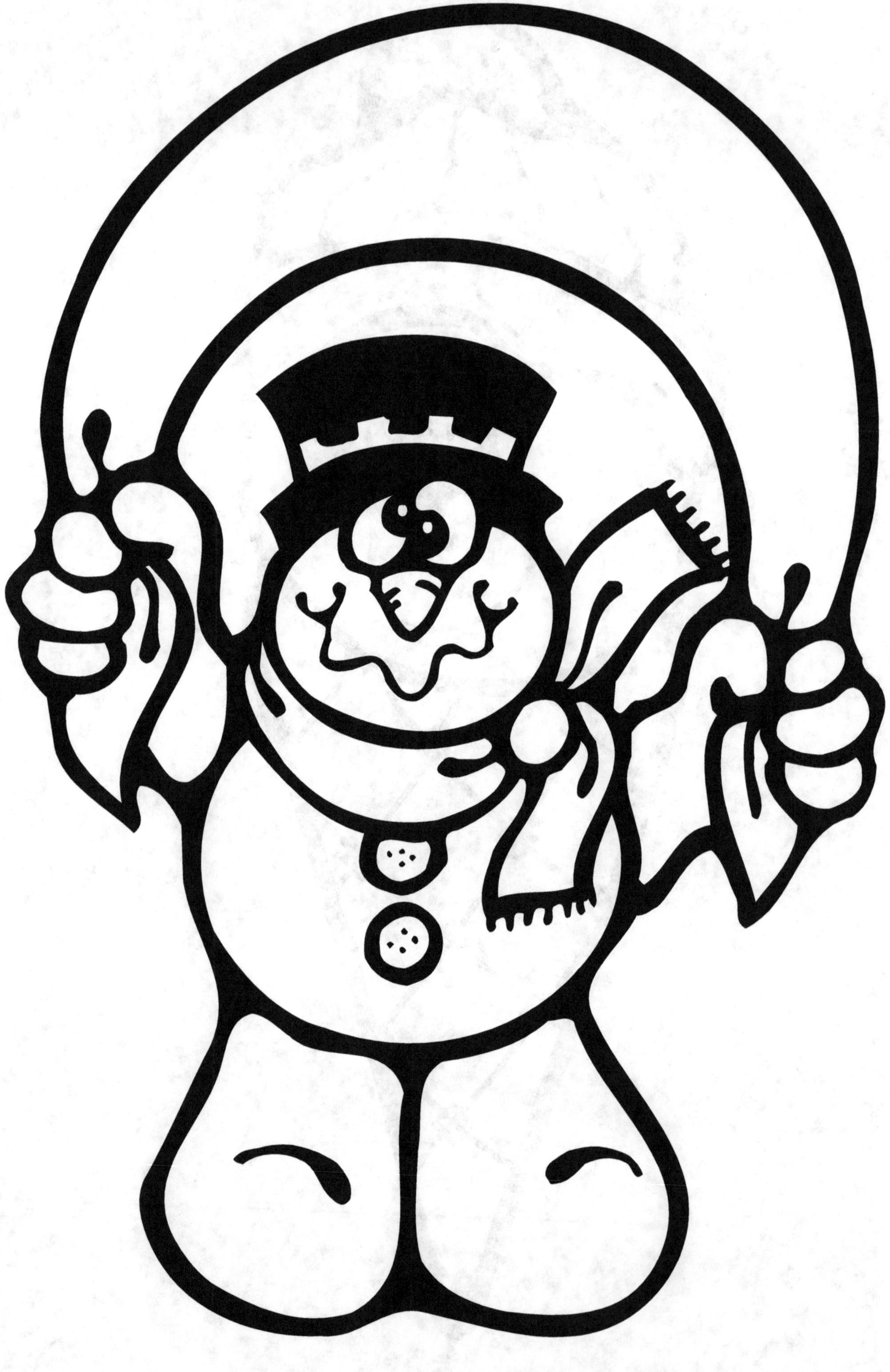

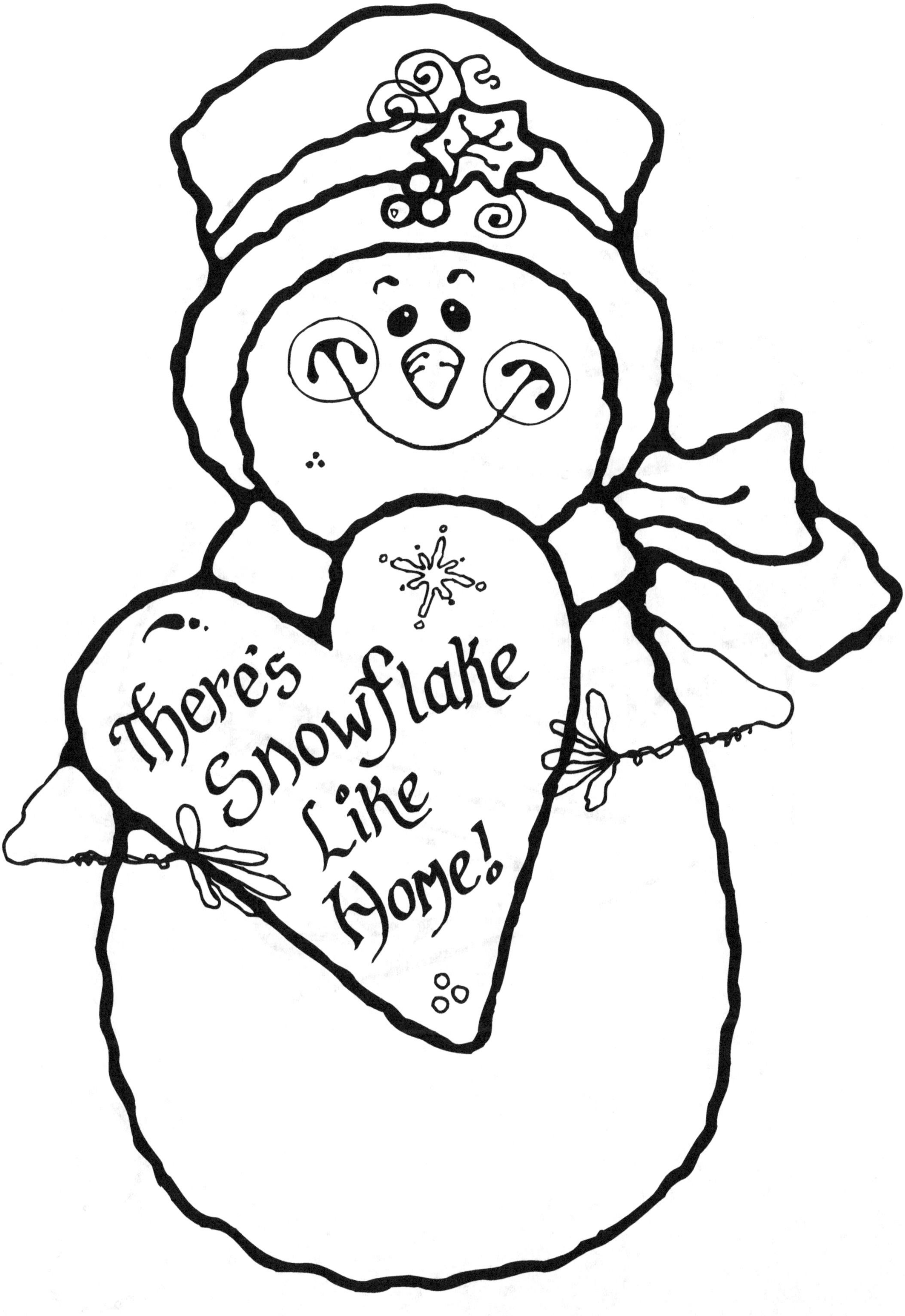
There's Snowflake Like Home!

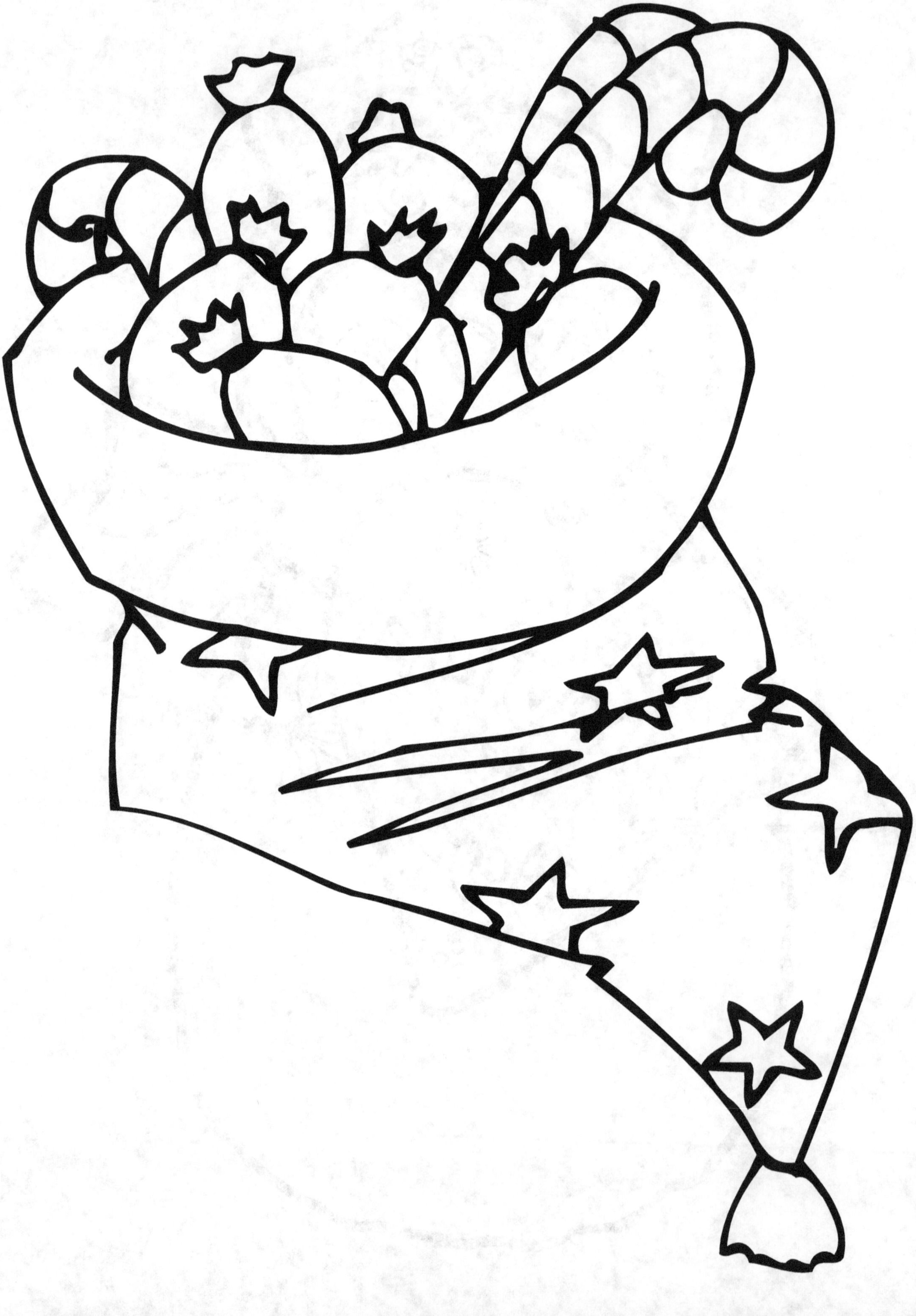

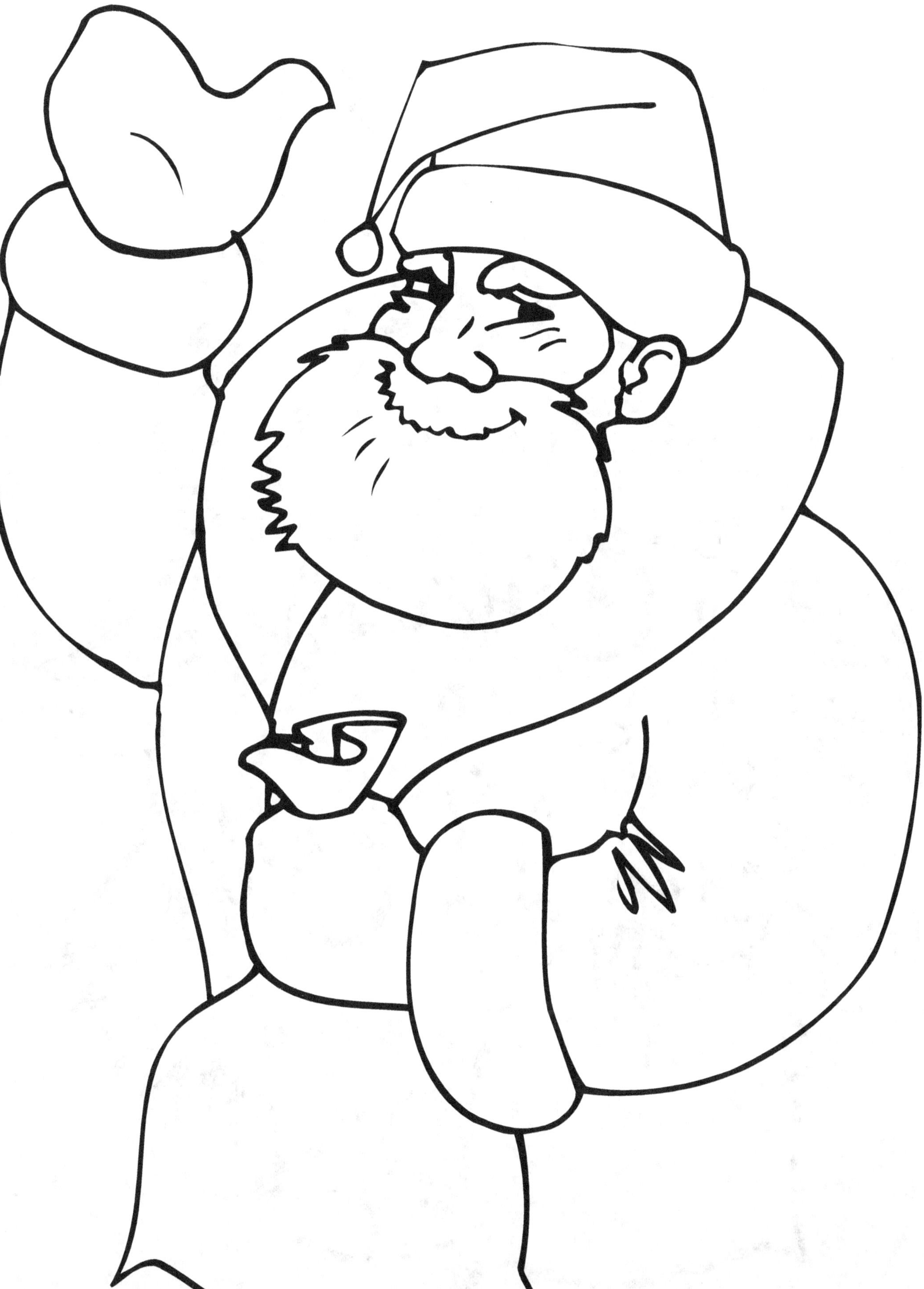

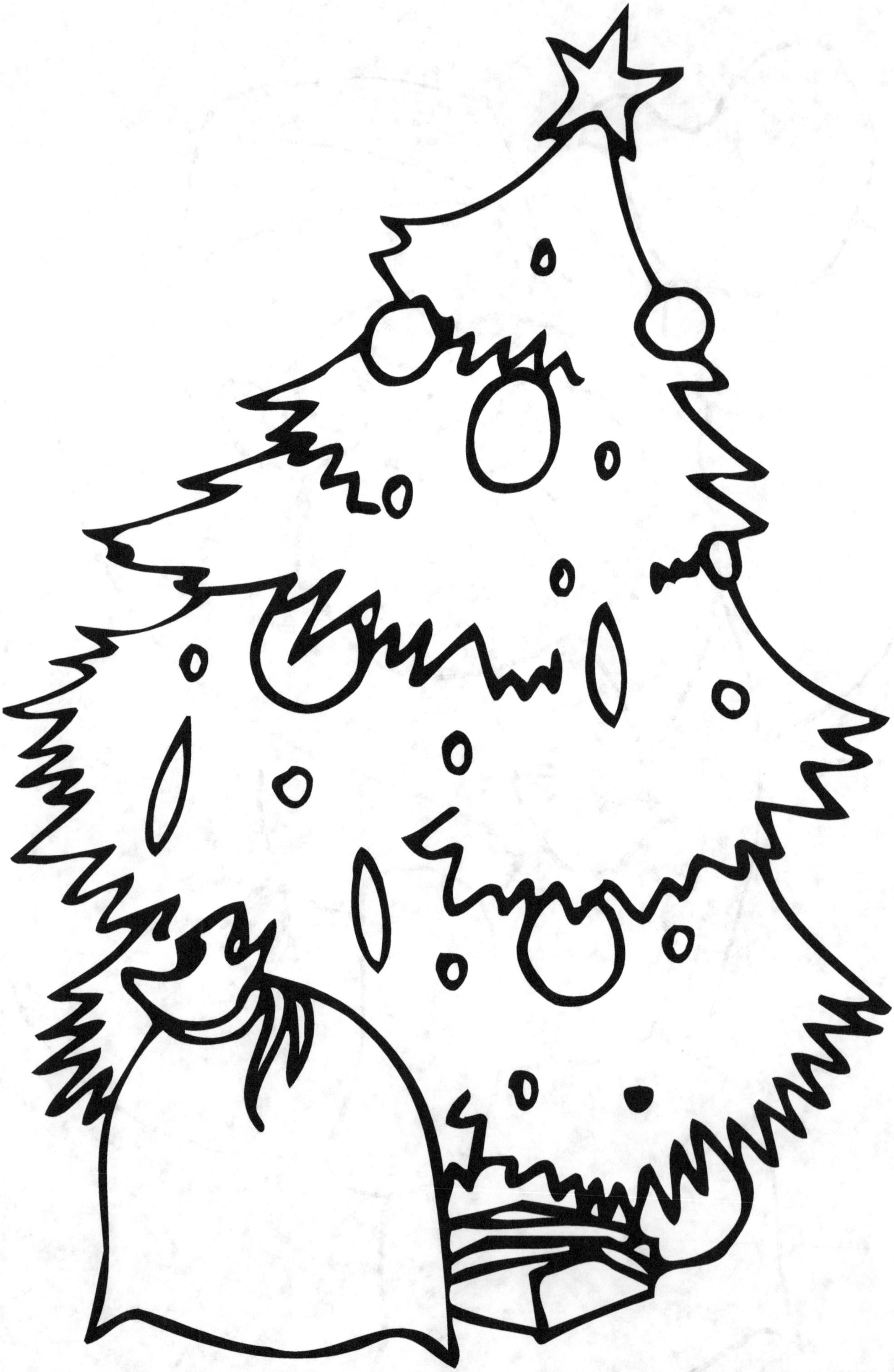

www.ingramcontent.com/pod-product-compliance
Lightning Source LLC
Chambersburg PA
CBHW081256180526
45170CB00007B/2457
* 9 7 8 1 5 4 0 3 6 8 3 6 2 *